INTEGRITY'S

iWORSH!P

A TOTAL WORSHIP EXPERIENCE

presents

DESPERATE FOR YOU

A 30-Day Worship Adventure

Roberta Croteau

DESPERATE FOR YOU

Devotions copyright © 2003 by Roberta Croteau.

Published by Integrity Publishers, a division of Integrity Media, Inc.,
5250 Virginia Way, Suite 100, Brentwood TN 37027.

HELPING PEOPLE WORLDWIDE EXPERIENCE *the* MANIFEST PRESENCE *of* GOD.

Cover Design: The Office of Bill Chiaravalle / www.officeofbc.com
Interior Design: Susan Browne Design, Nashville TN

ISBN 1-59145-053-5

Printed in the United States of America
03 04 05 06 07 RRD 9 8 7 6 5 4 3 2 1

TABLE OF CONTENTS

FOREWORD / *Breathe* 6

DAY ONE / LEAP / *Come, Now Is the Time to Worship* 9

DAY TWO / SEEK / *Hallelujah (Your Love Is Amazing)* 15

DAY THREE / EMBRACE / *He Knows My Name* 21

DAY FOUR / MEASURE / *Above All* 27

DAY FIVE / GIVE / *You Shine* 33

DAY SIX / MARVEL / *My Redeemer Lives* 39

DAY SEVEN / FLY / *Let It Rise* 45

DAY EIGHT / LOOK / *As the Deer* 51

DAY NINE / ILLUMINATE / *Shout to the Lord* 57

DAY TEN / PRAISE / *God of Wonders* 63

DAY ELEVEN / REMEMBER / *We Speak to Nations* 69

DAY TWELVE / DARE / *We All Bow Down* 75

DAY THIRTEEN / BELIEVE / *Blessed Assurance* 81

DAY FOURTEEN / RUN / *All Hail the Pow'r of Jesus' Name* 87

DAY FIFTEEN / CELEBRATE / *Grace Alone* 93

DAY SIXTEEN / WORSHIP / *Be Unto Your Name* 99

DAY SEVENTEEN / FOLLOW / *Every Move I Make* 105

DAY EIGHTEEN / GRASP / *You're Worthy of My Praise* 111

DAY NINETEEN / BEGIN / *That's Why We Praise Him* 117

DAY TWENTY / RETURN / *Sing for Joy* 123

DAY TWENTY-ONE / TRUST / *What a Friend I've Found* 129

DAY TWENTY-TWO / INVITE / *Open the Eyes of My Heart* 135

DAY TWENTY-THREE / LOVE / *Redeemer Savior Friend* 141

DAY TWENTY-FOUR / PERSEVERE / *Trading My Sorrows* 147

DAY TWENTY-FIVE / IMAGINE / *Awesome God* 153

DAY TWENTY-SIX / HOPE / *Let the River Flow* 159

DAY TWENTY-SEVEN / KNOW / *Knowing You (All I Once Held Dear)* . . . 165

DAY TWENTY-EIGHT / WALK / *I Will Sing* 171

DAY TWENTY-NINE / BECOME / *Days of Elijah* 177

DAY THIRTY / WISH / *Lord, I Lift Your Name On High* 183

LIFE IS
WORSHIP.
LET THE
ADVENTURE
BEGIN . . .

Breathe

Marie Barnett

This is the air I breathe
This is the air I breathe
Your holy presence living in me
This is my daily bread
This is my daily bread
Your very Word spoken to me
And I
I'm desperate for You
And I
I'm lost without You.

I THINK IT WAS THOREAU WHO FIRST ACCUSED US ALL OF LIVING LIVES OF QUIET DESPERATION. AND I DON'T THINK HE MEANT IT IN A GOOD WAY. FACT IS, MOST OF US WOULD SAY WE SEEK TO LIVE VERY UN-DESPERATE LIVES IF GIVEN THE OPTION.

But there's more to it than that. Desperate people are passionate people. If you don't want something badly enough, desperately enough—you just don't have the wherewithal to actually get it. Desperation can drive us almost as much as it can drive us crazy. It's a fine, fine line. But probably the most worthwhile one we ever walk.

If you've ever had that ceaseless ache in the center of your heart, you know the depths of the word *desperate*. Desperate people ache for fulfillment. And they'll go to any lengths to get it.

Ever been desperately in love? Then you know the deep desire to know someone more. And the lengths you'll go to get there. Desperately seeking answers? That's the only thing that could ever commit us to passionate searches. God desperately longs for us to seek Him. It's the paradox of all our lives. He wants us as much as we want Him. What better inspiration for the journey?

Desperation is the crux of worship. It's our daily longing to know God more, to know ourselves more, to live lives of fullness and wonder. It's the core of our being desperately reaching to our Creator—the only one who can reach us where we are and bring us everything we want, dream of, need.

As you begin this adventure in worship—this 30-day walk toward and through our desperation—I hope you'll find inspiration in the words of others walking this same road. And as you read of their journeys, you too can find your own voice and discover the signposts marking your own life as you take the time to journal your own thoughts, feelings, and insights along the way. At the end, may you still be desperate. May your journey be a never-ending run toward the One waiting desperately to hold you in His arms, teach you His ways, and love you into being the soul you were always meant to be . . .

Happy trails.

LEAP

LEAP

"IT IS GOOD TO PRAISE THE LORD AND
MAKE MUSIC TO YOUR NAME, O MOST HIGH,
TO PROCLAIM YOUR LOVE IN THE MORNING AND
YOUR FAITHFULNESS AT NIGHT..."

PSALM 92:1-2

Come, Now Is the Time to Worship

Brian Doerksen

Come, now is the time to worship
Come, now is the time to give your heart
Come, just as you are to worship
Come, just as you are before your God
Come

One day every tongue will confess You are God
One day every knee will bow
Still the greatest treasure remains for those
Who gladly choose You now

Willingly we choose to surrender our lives
Willingly our knees will bow
With all our heart, soul, mind, and strength
We gladly choose You now

IF WE WAIT FOR THE TIME WHEN EVERYTHING IS JUST RIGHT, WE WILL NEVER BEGIN.

This is true in love, in work, in art, in anything we ever need to attempt. I am the queen of procrastinators both in matters of the day and matters of the soul. I can put off sweeping a floor or making a bed longer (and more creatively) than anyone I've known. And like one writer wrote, I too enjoy the whooshing sound deadlines make as they go by. In matters of the soul I can convince myself that I will engage more profoundly and passionately with my Creator, "once I have Him all figured out." Why dive into an hour of prayer if you're still not quite sure just how God works things through? Sometimes, though, you just have to choose to begin.

"Leap and the net will appear," we are

I WORSHIP
because I can't help it. The more I understand about the overwhelming love and
grace of God that compelled Him to
place the very Lamb of God into the body
of a teenage girl, to be born into a culture
and time that would hound Him at every
turn, that would allow Him to be nailed to
the nightmare of our sinful lives all for love
of His lost sheep, the more I cry Holy, Holy,
Holy is the Lamb. Knowledge that doesn't
lead to worship is empty. The whole
purpose of my life is love, loving Him.
—*Sheila Walsh; Artist, Author, Speaker*

promised. All we have to do is take that first step off the ledge. Boldness does have a certain magic to it. It's something that goes way beyond "if you can see it, you can be it"—although I have no doubt that that is true as well. A leap of faith requires more than just a jump; it requires the ability to absolutely let go of everything that's keeping us on the ledge, including that voice that says it just can't be done.

If we feel we have to wait for just the right time and place to come and worship, we have yet to discover the real freedom of worship. Now isn't necessarily the time to worship because every moment is the time to worship. We are called to passionately embrace our God at every turn, through every minute, and in every way possible. If music is your worship, sing loudly. If service is your worship, serve extravagantly. If just being is your worship, live boldly. Jump into worship as bravely as you can jump into life, because the reality is, they are one and the same. Living every moment for the glory of God and to the glory of God is a never-ending adventure that, once begun,

---

WE ARE CALLED TO PASSIONATELY EMBRACE OUR GOD AT EVERY TURN, THROUGH EVERY MINUTE, AND IN EVERY WAY POSSIBLE.

---

you'll never want to end. Don't wait until the moment is just right or you'll spend your life sitting on the shore watching for that never-to-come perfect wave. *Carpe diem,* as they say. Seize every moment and dive on in. The water's fine.

WHAT KEEPS YOU FROM LETTING GO OF EVERYTHING AND TRULY
WORSHIPING GOD? TRY TO RECOUNT ALL OF THE EXCUSES, EVEN THE
HIDDEN ONES, THAT HAVE MADE YOU "PUT OFF" GIVING ALL TO HIM.

SEEK

DAY TWO

SEEK

"NEITHER A LOFTY DEGREE OF INTELLIGENCE
NOR IMAGINATION NOR BOTH TOGETHER
GO TO THE MAKING OF GENIUS. LOVE, LOVE, LOVE,
THAT IS THE SOUL OF GENIUS."

MOZART

Hallelujah (Your Love Is Amazing)
Brenton Brown and Brian Doerksen

Hallelujah, hallelujah, hallelujah
Your love makes me sing
Hallelujah, hallelujah, hallelujah
Your love makes me sing

Your love is surprising, I can feel it rising
All the joy that's growing deep inside of me
Every time I see You, all Your goodness shines through
I can feel this Godsong rising up in me

Your love is amazing, steady and unchanging
Your love is a mountain firm beneath my feet
Your love is a mystery how You gently lift me
When I am discouraged Your love carries me

THE COSMONAUT
LANDED HIS CAPSULE
BRAVELY BACK ON
EARTH AND
DECLARED THERE
WAS NO GOD.

He had
sailed through
the heavens and
saw no sign of Him. Too bad they didn't send
up a poet—he would have seen God everywhere.

Through the centuries scientists and artists
have searched for God, each in his own way.
One sits in a lab and waits for the smoke to
clear to find the proof; the other sits with pen
in hand and finds Him in the fog.

And even though He is the one who set
the atoms abuzz and swung the cosmos into
orbit and designed all the ebb and flow of life
within and without us, I still think God is

more poet than scientist.

I have yet to understand the science of God. I can't prove Him there; I can't understand His logic—sometimes it takes everything within just to believe He might really be.

The poetry of God I do see. I can fathom the epic truth of love degrading a Creator enough to step in for the death scene. I can see the rhyme, even when I can't see the reason. Love is an amazing catalyst. It can send mere mortals to reach for unimaginable heights. It brought the Maker of the Universe down to an unimaginable depth.

"For God so loved the world" is the beginning of poetry—when the old world started dying, the new world began. He is the poet who sees the promise of life in the ashes and the artist who can find the starlight in an empty sky.

His science is too expansive for me to embrace, but I can see His art in every atom, hear it in every sound, feel it in every heartbeat.

HE IS THE POET WHO SEES THE PROMISE OF LIFE IN THE ASHES AND THE ARTIST WHO CAN FIND THE STARLIGHT IN AN EMPTY SKY.

I guess it's not so strange that the wanderers who watched the sky and followed the road under it are forever remembered as "wise men." Their wealth of wisdom didn't stop them from taking on the quite illogical task of following one bright star through the dark, cold nights of foreign lands. And their reward was to find what the whole world seeks—

God in a box—proof you can touch, a flesh-and-bone stranger who knows them more than they know themselves.

And that same singer, dancer, poet, painter of earth and heaven still flings Himself across a million miles of sky. Send up any contraption you want to search for the place He lives and you'll still come back empty-handed like the cosmonaut. But I'll bet you God was there all right, dancing in His heavens. And if you had looked with more than your eyes, you just might have seen Him there.

YOUR WORSHIP
ADVENTURE

THINK ABOUT ALL THE AMAZING WAYS GOD HAS LOVED YOU.
WRITE DOWN JUST ONE OF THE STORIES THAT YOU'VE TOLD TO EXPLAIN
IT WHENEVER SOMEONE ASKS YOU WHY YOU BELIEVE.

_____

_____

_____

_____

_____

_____

_____

_____

_____

_____

_____

_____

_____

_____

_____

_____

EMBRACE

EMBRACE

"HOW GOD WORKS IN ANSWER TO PRAYER
IS A MYSTERY THAT LOGIC CANNOT PENETRATE,
BUT THAT HE DOES WORK IN ANSWER
TO PRAYER IS GLORIOUSLY TRUE."

OSWALD CHAMBERS

He Knows My Name
Tommy Walker

I have a Maker
He formed my heart
Before even time began
My life was in His hand

He knows my name
He knows my every thought
He sees each tear that falls
And hears me when I call

I have a Father
He calls me His own
He'll never leave me
No matter where I go

I RECENTLY READ A BOOK THAT HAD A POIGNANT SCENE BETWEEN A BELIEVER GRAPPLING WITH UNBELIEF AND DESPAIR AND HIS JOB-LIKE FRIEND TRYING TO CONVINCE HIM EVERYTHING WAS OKAY. "There is not one sparrow that falls that God doesn't know about," he offers as a comfort. "Yes," his desperate friend counters back, "but the sparrow still falls."

How many times have we lost comfort in the fact that God sees and knows, and yet doesn't seem to do anything about our circumstance? We still get lost, bleed, cry, die . . . what does it really matter that God saw it all if He didn't do anything about it? We are prompted by Jesus' very words to watch the lilies as they grow in splendor and know that His very hand coaxed them out of the ground. How much more can He make something beautiful of our lives? And yet there is still so much ugliness, so much pain—where can we find that peace that passes understanding when all we understand is that everything is going wrong?

I don't have an answer. It's a prayer I grapple with daily. And so far the only way that I have found toward the light is to embrace the mystery. There's an old Sunday school lesson that has us consider a tapestry. When you look at it from the back, you wonder what's going on. There are bumps and knots and crisscrossing yarns that make no sense at all. It's all one chaotic mess. But when you turn it over and look at how the colors and threads come together in one beautiful picture, you

---

SUDDENLY YOU BEGIN TO REALIZE THAT WHAT WAS UGLY ON THE BACK WAS NECESSARY TO MAKE SOMETHING BEAUTIFUL ON THE FRONT.

---

start to understand the back. The lines had to cross, the knots had to form, the threads had to dangle. Suddenly you begin to realize that what was ugly on the back was necessary to make something beautiful on the front. This is what I hold on to. I will never understand all the bumps and knots and dangling threads that life seems to create—but I can believe that it all has a reason. That somehow it all has meaning. Even if I'll never see it on this side of life's tapestry.

And since we walk by faith and not by sight, we have to continue the journey with the simple trust that God is in His heaven and all is right with our world. Ultimately, His ways are not our ways, but miraculously, He sometimes allows us a passing glance at what might be . . . and what we might become. And His eye is always on the sparrow, no matter where it may fly or fall.

YOUR WORSHIP
ADVENTURE

THINK OF ONE OF THE MORE PAINFUL OR "UGLY" MOMENTS IN YOUR
LIFE. SEE IF YOU CAN "TURN IT OVER AND LOOK AT THE FRONT"
NOW THAT SOME TIME HAS PASSED. CAN YOU FIND SOMETHING
BEAUTIFUL IN SOMETHING THAT ONCE WAS ANYTHING BUT?

JOURNAL

MEASURE

MEASURE

"WHO, BEING IN VERY NATURE GOD, DID NOT
CONSIDER EQUALITY WITH GOD SOMETHING
TO BE GRASPED, BUT MADE HIMSELF NOTHING,
TAKING THE VERY NATURE OF A SERVANT,
BEING MADE IN HUMAN LIKENESS."

PHILIPPIANS 2:6-7

Above All
Paul Baloche and Lenny LeBlanc

*Above all powers, above all kings
Above all nature and all created things
Above all wisdom and all the ways of man
You were here before the world began*

*Above all kingdoms, above all thrones
Above all wonders the world has ever known
Above all wealth and treasures of the earth
There's no way to measure what You're worth*

*Crucified, laid behind a stone
You lived to die rejected and alone
Like a rose trampled on the ground
You took the fall and thought of me
Above all*

ABOVE ALL

WORDS FROM THE SONGWRITER
LENNY LEBLANC

GOD IS ABOVE ALL POWERS AND ALL KINGS. Psalm 95:3 says, "For the LORD is the great God, the great King above all gods." From the beginning of time there has not been a leader or a king who has even come close to affecting the world in the way that Jesus Christ has. Two thousand years after His death, burial, and resurrection, the lives of millions of people continue to be transformed as they receive His love and forgiveness. HE IS ABOVE ALL NATURE AND ALL CREATED THINGS. In the first chapter of Romans, Paul talks about how God has revealed His eternal power and divine nature through the beauty of His creation, and so man has no excuse for not acknowledging Him. HE IS ABOVE ALL WISDOM AND ALL THE WAYS OF MAN. The scriptures are many that say God's wisdom is greater and His ways are higher than ours. HE IS ABOVE ALL KINGDOMS, ABOVE ALL THRONES. Our Lord's Kingdom is not of this world, but as His children we've been given a deposit of His heavenly Kingdom here on earth. HE IS ABOVE ALL WONDERS THE WORLD HAS EVER KNOWN. In my travels I've had the privilege of seeing some beautiful places. Sometimes I'll try to describe the wonder of what I saw to my family and friends, but somehow I always seem to come up short. Most of us have never actually seen the Lord in the natural but we've all witnessed His grace and mercy, both personally and through each other. That kind of beauty far surpasses anything I've ever laid eyes on or experienced. HE IS ABOVE ALL WEALTH AND TREASURES OF THE EARTH. Many people live their whole lives trying to gain wealth and fame, hoping that they will be fulfilled, when all the while the One who can quench their endless thirst and *hunger stands waiting with arms open wide. His undying love is the most precious jewel of all.* THERE'S NO WAY TO MEASURE WHAT YOU'RE WORTH. *There is simply no unit of measurement we could use to calculate the worth of our Lord. How can you even begin to assess the value of the One who spoke the universe into existence?*

CRUCIFIED, LAID BEHIND A STONE. *Here is where my words take a dramatic turn. It seems like after all that's been said about His worth and His supremacy, we should now say He is worthy, holy, and so majestic. But wait. Look at what our Lord allowed to happen.* YOU LIVED TO DIE REJECTED AND ALONE. *Jesus' sole purpose was to do the will of the Father, even to the point of dying and being rejected by the ones He came to save.* LIKE A ROSE TRAMPLED ON THE GROUND. *Those seven words only begin to portray how something so pure and beautiful could be so crudely discarded by the very ones to whom the gift was given.* YOU TOOK THE FALL AND THOUGHT OF ME ABOVE ALL. *Oh Father in heaven, how great is Your love for us, that You would give the dearest thing to Your heart as a sacrifice for the sins of mankind that we might know You and have relationship with You. Help us, Lord, to somehow understand the weight of what You did for us. May we surrender our hearts and forever place You . . . Above All.*

Lenny LeBlanc is no stranger to creating memorable songs. In his early career he had a mainstream megahit with the rock classic "Falling." After turning his life over to God, Lenny found a new career as a Christian artist and became deeply involved in his church's music program, eventually joining the staff as musical director. Lenny has created some of the most popular worship standards of the modern church, including "Above All," a song that was recorded by Christian music giant Michael W. Smith and became an across-the-board, number one hit.

WHAT IS THE NUMBER ONE PRIORITY IN YOUR LIFE RIGHT NOW?
COULD YOU EVER GIVE IT ALL UP FOR SOMEONE ELSE? FOR GOD?
THINK ABOUT WHAT YOU PRIZE MOST IN YOUR LIFE AND REFLECT ON
HOW GOD GAVE WHAT HE PRIZED MOST FOR YOU. IN WHAT SMALL WAYS
CAN YOU TRY TO REPAY THAT FAVOR?

JOURNAL

GIVE
DAY FIVE
GIVE

"It has never been quite enough to say that God is in his heaven and all is right with the world, since the rumor that God had left his heavens to set it right."

G. K. CHESTERTON

You Shine
Brian Doerksen

Why should I fear man
When You made the heavens?
Why should I be afraid
When You put the stars in place?
Why should I lose heart
When I know how great You are?
Why should I give up
When Your plans are full of love?
In this world we will have trouble
But You have overcome the world.

You shine
Brighter than the brightest star.
You love
Purer than the purest heart.
You shine
Filling us with courage and strength
To follow You.

"FOOLISH CHILDREN IN A FLAT" IS WHAT O. HENRY CALLED THEM—THE HERO AND HEROINE OF HIS LITTLE CHRISTMAS TALE THAT WRAPPED UP THE TRUE SPIRIT OF THE SEASON.

Remember the story? She cut off her hair to buy him a watch chain, but while she wasn't looking, he sold his watch to buy her hair combs. And when the story ends, you see a young man and a young woman, desperately poor and desperately in love, staring at the two useless gifts in their hands.

Ah, but of course, that's not really the end of the story. And the gifts weren't really useless.

True, she had no hair left to wrap up in the shiny combs, and he had no watch left to hang on the platinum chain. But who of us— if we possessed the love within this couple— would have traded those brown paper and tinsel-wrapped boxes for all the treasure in the world?

And when those first wise men arrived on the Christmas scene bearing gold and frankincense and myrrh to leave at the Messiah-child's feet—what really were the gifts of the Magi? A sack of gold and some fancy perfume? Or the faith-filled trek that brought them there in the first place? What does a poor carpenter's family do with gifts fit for a king? What does a poor couple do with a couple of expensive trinkets?

When love jumps ahead of all reason,

when we and our hearts and our God become fools for love—there's the gift to keep. Three men leaving their lives behind to see what fell from the stars, and two young lovers giving what was most precious to the one they

---

AND YOU CAN STILL KNOW THAT HIS LOVE IS AS SPONTANEOUS AND EXTRAVAGANT AND FOOLISH AS THAT OF THE WISE MEN AND THE LOVERS.

---

found even more precious—this is the love that makes everything else pale.

And even in our darkest hours—when you walk through the world and see that love doesn't always last, and that justice doesn't always prevail, and that dreams often die in the gutter, and that the innocent still die while the guilty go free—then you must know . . .

Know that you can still see that star burning in the east. You can still look into the window of a tiny New York apartment and glimpse the glow of love. And you can still know that His love is as spontaneous and extravagant and foolish as that of the wise men and the lovers.

He who owned the world cut Himself from the very net of heaven to buy it back. And we who have so little to offer must become as foolish as He (after all, God has chosen the foolish of the world to confound the wise) and freely sell what precious little life we can for a tiny piece of that mad God's dream.

YOUR WORSHIP
ADVENTURE

HAVE YOU EVER BEEN FOOLISHLY EXTRAVAGANT WITH YOUR LOVE?
WHAT'S THE WILDEST THING YOU EVER DID FOR SOMEONE—OR WHAT
DO YOU WISH YOU COULD DO FOR SOMEONE? MAKE IT YOUR GOAL
THIS DAY TO FIND A WAY TO DO IT AGAIN—OR DISCOVER
THE JOY OF DOING IT FOR THE FIRST TIME!

JOURNAL

MARVEL

MARVEL

"I KNOW THAT MY REDEEMER LIVES, AND THAT
IN THE END HE WILL STAND UPON THE EARTH."

JOB 19:25

My Redeemer Lives

Reuben Morgan

I know He's rescued my soul
His blood covered my sin
I believe, I believe
My shame He's taken away
My pain is healed in His name
I believe, I believe

I'll raise a banner
'Cause my Lord has conquered the grave
My Redeemer lives, my Redeemer lives
My Redeemer lives, my Redeemer lives

You lift my burden
I'll rise with You
I'm dancing on this mountaintop
To see Your kingdom come

I LOVE THIS STORY.
IT'S SO GOOD, I HATE
TO ADMIT, THAT I
FEAR IT MAY BE ONE
OF THOSE URBAN
LEGEND THINGS
THAT DIDN'T
REALLY HAPPEN.

But like any good legend, of course, it *could* have happened, and that's all that really matters . . .

A woman called into a radio program where the brave host tackled tough questions on the Bible. The earnest caller implored the host to explain how on earth some Christians could condone drinking alcohol when the Bible clearly taught that such activity was not acceptable. The host pointed to several verses and the story of Jesus at the wedding in particular. There He turned water into wine. And on other occasions He quite clearly imbibed. "But surely that was just grape juice," the caller countered. Well, not so, the host adroitly countered back. He then speedily

> I WORSHIP
> because worship places me in the right posture before God.
> ---*Max Lucado, Author*

offered more proof that many of Jesus' potables were in fact potent. He was of the opinion that, in no uncertain terms, drinking wine was an activity Jesus and His followers engaged in. At the end of her list of questions on the topic, convinced that the radio host was probably right, the shattered woman finally proclaimed, "How could our Lord *do* that?"

I still laugh every time I hear the story. It's so easy to get caught up in what we believe, we forget where the truth originates—and sometimes what the truth originally looked like. But before I laugh too much at her, I try to remember that every one of us has our own comfortable litany of laws and lessons we live by. Curbing someone else's dogma is easy; stuffing a sock in your own can be downright painful.

So much of the joy that comes from believing, for me, has been all the times I discovered I was wrong. Jesus was as astounding to the men and women He touched on earth as He is to us every day we earnestly seek Him. He told them, and He tells us—listen, everything you thought you knew? You were wrong. Blissfully wrong.

You thought you were unlovable? Look at My scars. You thought no one was listening to your prayers? Just watch what comes next. You thought you'd never make it through another day? Look at every angel in disguise I sent to you through the faces and hands of those you love, and even some you didn't know you loved. Every moment that we're paying attention He calls to us and says, Why don't you try looking at it this way this time? If you thought that was amazing, just wait'll you see this!

Two wrongs may not make a right, but in God's arithmetic of love, He can make anything add up. One sinner with a price on his head plus one Savior with a life to give makes everything. How could our Lord do *that*?

YOUR WORSHIP
ADVENTURE

Think of something you passionately believe in. Now imagine for a moment that you are wrong. What would you do?

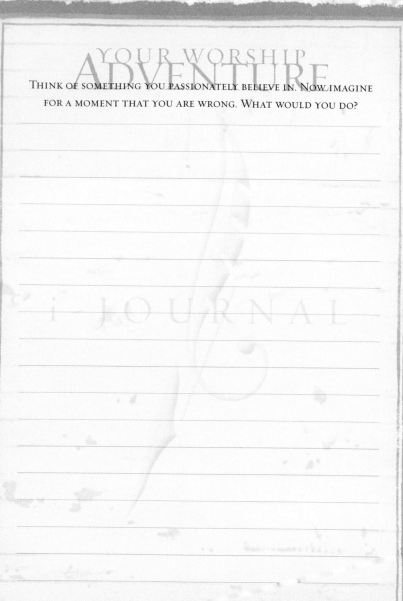

DAY SEVEN
FLY

> "SET ME FREE FROM MY PRISON,
> THAT I MAY PRAISE YOUR NAME."

PSALM 142:7

Let It Rise
Holland Davis

Let the glory of the Lord
Rise among us
Let the glory of the Lord
Rise among us
Let the praises of the King
Rise among us
Let it rise

Let the songs of the Lord
Rise among us
Let the songs of the Lord
Rise among us
Let the joy of the king
Rise among us
Let it rise
O let it rise

THERE IS A
WONDERFUL FABLE
FOUND IN THOSE
In the story
COLORFUL, ALBEIT
a young Jesus is
VERY DEBATABLE,
working at His
"LOST GOSPELS"
father's carpentry
SURROUNDING
shop and gently
THE EARLY YEARS
carving delicate
OF JESUS' LIFE.

birds from the strewn scraps of wood on the
floor. Then, in one glorious swoop, He leans out
the window and flings His wooden creations
into the air. And in stunning fairy-tale fashion,
the wooden wings spring to feathery life and
take to the skies. The works of His hands break
free from the laws of the earth and gravity
and explode into new life in the wild blue

yonder. And even as He lets go, you know
that His letting go is really just the birth of
something better than anyone ever expected.

I WORSHIP

(at least I wish to!) with every breath, every
thought, every endeavor and every longing
of my heart. True worship surely should be
total! As a "true worshiper" (John 4.21-23), if my
worship flows out of my relationship with a
Father who loves me unconditionally, then it
surely would be foolish to do anything
without reference to the One who gave
me everything at the inconceivable cost of
His own Glorious Son, and ultimately all for
His glory and not mine! Though incredibly
His glory brings me more pleasure than
anything else in this world.

—*Paul Oakley, Worship Leader and Songwriter*

I'm not enough of a Bible scholar to
know why and how this story never made

the final cut, but I do know that it wouldn't throw me one bit to discover it actually happened. Why not? What a picture of Jesus' tenderness and artful desire to see anything He's created be beautiful and free!

WHAT A PICTURE OF JESUS' TENDERNESS AND ARTFUL DESIRE TO SEE ANYTHING HE'S CREATED BE BEAUTIFUL AND FREE!

"According to most philosophers," writes Chesterton, "God, in making the world, enslaved it. According to Christianity, in making it, He set it free." Yes. God continually recreates us out of the mess of ourselves left trampled and forgotten on unswept floors.

And instead of letting us collect dust on a shelf, He tosses us out into the glorious unknown.

Every creation is a separation. Everything you make will never have life until you let it go. And God apparently knows that better than anyone. Everything He's ever made, He's set free—even when he knew He risked it never coming back at all. He always takes the chance. He will always believe that what He sends out in love can come back to the love that dared to let it fly in the first place. And those tender, skillful hands that beautifully molded and knit you together before you even had a name, are the same hands that lift you up to the skies and give you wings. And they are the same arms that reach out with joy and lovingly await your return.

HAVE YOU EVER HAD TO LET GO OF SOMEONE OR SOMETHING?
WAS THE PAIN OF THAT SEPARATION WORTH WHATEVER BECAME OF IT?
WOULD YOU OR COULD YOU DO IT AGAIN?

JOURNAL

LOOK

LOOK

"THOSE WHO BELIEVE THEY BELIEVE IN GOD,
BUT WITHOUT PASSION IN THE HEART, WITHOUT
ANGUISH OF MIND, WITHOUT UNCERTAINTY,
WITHOUT DOUBT, AND EVEN AT TIMES WITHOUT
DESPAIR, BELIEVE ONLY IN THE IDEA OF GOD,
AND NOT IN GOD HIMSELF."

MIGUEL DE UNAMUNO

As the Deer
Martin Nystrom

As the deer pants for the water
So my soul longs after You
You alone are my heart's desire
And I long to worship You

You alone are my strength, my shield
To You alone may my spirit yield
You alone are my heart's desire
And I long to worship You

I want you more than gold or silver
Only you can satisfy
You alone are the real joygiver
And the apple of my eye

EIGHT

POOR OLD
WILE E. COYOTE.
HOW MANY
zillion SATURDAY
MORNINGS HAS HE
SPENT HOPELESSLY
TRYING TO CATCH
THE ROAD RUNNER?

How many times have we watched him open yet another ACME package and put together a ridiculous contraption, only to miss netting, yet again, that elusive bird?

How many times have we watched ourselves open yet another package of hope and put together a clever contraption of our own devices, only to miss netting, again and again, the elusive shreds of our faith and the truth that dangles on every end?

Everyone clings to the dream of knowing

"the answer" as if actually knowing the answer might really be a cure-all. "Show us a miracle; give us a sign," the dogging crowds hounded Him day after day as He gave thirty-three of His eternal years to letting us follow Him around. But the more we asked, the more He seemed silent. What is truth?—to which even Pilate himself received no answer, and what is the answer?—to which we all still wait and watch for a reply.

On her deathbed, author Gertrude Stein purportedly asked that universal question, "What is the answer?" When no answer came, she laughed and asked, "In that case, what is the question?" Famous last words.

Maybe it's not so strange that Jesus usually answered questions with another question. Maybe it's because it's not the answer that really matters, but the search itself that makes us who we are.

"To have found God and still to pursue Him is the soul's paradox of love," wrote A. W. Tozer. He, too, discovered that the joy may truly be on the road there, more than on the road back.

If you've ever taught a Sunday school class, you've probably discovered that most eager-to-please five-year-olds have quickly caught on to the idea that Jesus is the answer . . . to everything. Ask who crossed the Red Sea with the Israelites, who ran from God and was swept into the sea, or any other question, and you'll inevitably get a chorus of "Jesus" shouted back. They've figured out that Jesus is always the right answer. After all, how could a teacher ever say that Jesus isn't the answer? Problem is, both in Sunday school and in life, He very often is the problem more than He is the answer. But He is the only problem worth trying to solve and the only question worth trying to answer. And He is the only road ever worth taking.

The pursuit of the dream *does* mean more than the dream itself. Maybe even the Coyote's devilish plotting and planning makes his life more worth living than any one dished-up meal of Road Runner ever could. Maybe endlessly hunting for God, in the long run, is better than actually thinking we've captured Him.

I still haven't found what I'm looking for . . . but I think I'm starting to like it that way.

YOUR WORSHIP
ADVENTURE

IF YOU COULD BUILD YOUR OWN LIFE TO LIVE OVER AGAIN, WHAT
WOULD YOU CHANGE ABOUT YOURSELF? YOUR CIRCUMSTANCES?
WITHOUT THE POWER TO REALLY DO THAT, WHAT CAN YOU DO TODAY
TO MAKE YOUR LIFE CLOSER TO THE ONE YOU'VE JUST IMAGINED?

i-JOURNAL

ILLUMINATE

ILLUMINATE

"SHOUT FOR JOY TO THE LORD, ALL THE EARTH.
WORSHIP THE LORD WITH GLADNESS;
COME BEFORE HIM WITH JOYFUL SONGS."

—— PSALM 100:1-2

Shout to the Lord
Darlene Zschech

My Jesus, my Savior, Lord, there is none like You
All of my days I want to praise the wonders
of Your mighty love
My comfort, my shelter, tower of refuge and strength
Let every breath, all that I am, never cease
to worship You

Shout to the Lord, all the earth; let us sing
Power and majesty praise to the King
Mountains bow down and the seas will roar
At the sound of Your name
I sing for joy at the work of Your hands
Forever I'll love You, forever I'll stand
Nothing compares to the promise I have in You

INSIDE THIS SKIN, SOMEHOW, HIDDEN BELOW THE SURFACE, SCRAPING AND GASPING FOR LIFE AND BREATH, LIVES GOD.

He came in when I least expected it, when the welcome mat was muddy and worn—yet here He stays. "Into my heart, into my heart," we hear the children sing, "come into my heart, Lord Jesus." And sitting here too, in our older skin, we sing it and say it and try to believe it could possibly be true. True that the God of time and space and earth and fire and heaven, that the God of Abraham, Jacob, Joseph, and a mob of mad prophets might actually choose to nest in the chambers of our own hearts. It boggles the mind that Something so big could live in something so small—that Something so pure could rest in something so unworthy.

But there's the secret. He has made His temple here. Our bones are His very walls. And then the even greater mystery—not just God with us, God for us, and God in us, but God in us wholly. He who poured the universe into being does not portion out His entrance into human hearts. He comes completely. It is we who dilute Him, hide Him, lock Him so tightly inside that only on a few rare occasions does His presence there seem even a remote possibility.

The songwriters have described stars in the sky as holes in the floor of heaven. The glory of God shining down in specks and fragments. How much like us is that skin of dark sky, that floor of heaven holding in the Light of the World with only brief, broken bits piercing through.

I SEE SOMETIMES IN FITS AND STARTS THE WORKINGS OF A SPIRIT SO HOLY THAT FLESH SHUDDERS TO FEEL HIS POWER RUN THROUGH IT.

Could it be then that, just as that broken sky allows His light to bleed through, in our own lives His love shines through our wounds? "By His stripes we are healed," the Scriptures announce—and maybe it is through our own wounds that we give Him life on this earth. I see sometimes in fits and starts the workings of a Spirit so holy that flesh shudders to feel His power run through it. His light escapes our darkness—and even when our blood runs cold, still it is God who uses our hands, our feet, our hearts, our lives to pour His love into the world. Our only duty in this holy exchange seems to be a willingness to be used . . . and even without that, we know He could still use the rocks to tell His story.

But it is us whom He has chosen—and whether we are bruised by Him or by the world around us, we can only pray as one poet hoped, to "be wounded by our own understanding of love . . . and to bleed willingly and joyfully."

WHAT WOUNDS IN YOUR LIFE HAS GOD USED TO POUR
HIS LIGHT THROUGH TO OTHERS?

JOURNAL

PRAISE

DAY TEN

PRAISE

"O Lord, our Lord, how majestic is
your name in all the earth!"

PSALM 8:1, 3

God of Wonders
Marc Byrd and Steve Hindalong

Lord of all creation
Of water, earth and sky
The heavens are Your tabernacle
Glory to the Lord on high

God of wonders beyond our galaxy
You are holy, holy
The universe declares Your majesty
You are holy, holy
Lord of Heaven and earth

Early in the morning
I will celebrate the light
When I stumble in the darkness
I will call Your name by night

Hallelujah to the Lord of Heaven and earth

Precious Lord, reveal Your heart to me
Father, hold me, hold me
The universe declares Your majesty
You are holy, holy

GOD OF WONDERS

WORDS FROM THE SONGWRITER
STEVE HINDALONG

PRECIOUS LORD, REVEAL YOUR HEART TO ME.
FATHER, HOLD ME, HOLD ME . . .

On the morning of September 18, 1988, I held my
newborn child, Emily, for the first time. That's when
the word "love" took on intensely new meaning for me.
As I cradled my daughter in my arms, singing to her a
freshly invented little ditty, I realized like never before—
vulnerability . . . joy near dread . . . a wonderful ache . . .
unconditional love. Yes, and in parenthood, I dare say,
I've gained profound insight concerning the heart of
Holy God—Abba—our heavenly Father. He created
us to be intimate with Him, and in so doing took
great risk. He loves us, His children, so passionately!
"And so we know and rely on the love God has for us.

God is Love . . ." (1 John 4:16).

Erin and Emily are twelve and fourteen now, and
. . . well, they confound me a good bit. They're girls and
. . . like I said, they're twelve and fourteen. Try as I
may, it seems lately there's not a lot I can do or say to fix
their troubles, or to protect their hearts from hurt.
And I'm beginning to understand that much of the time
the best I can do is to listen closely . . . and hold them
tight. My love for my children is true, and I need them
to know it.

Surely, God desires that we feel such assurance.
He wants us to know that He accepts us exactly as we
are, and that His affection for us is infinite. Abba enjoys
our company and longs to spend time with us.

It's unfathomable, really. The majestic Lord of all
creation—of water, earth, and sky . . . ruler of the universe who ordains the sun to rise and fall . . . almighty

God of wonders beyond our galaxy—dwells in our very

midst . . . in spirit. He hears us when we call His name

I REALIZED LIKE NEVER
BEFORE—VULNERABILITY . . .
JOY NEAR DREAD . . .
A WONDERFUL ACHE . . .
UNCONDITIONAL LOVE.

---

by night. And when we stumble in the darkness, our

Father reaches for us with tender mercy. Our God is

light . . . He is holy . . . and He is love.

Hallelujah to the Lord of heaven and earth!

Together with his writing partner, Marc Byrd, Steve Hindalong could never have imagined that the little song they wrote one day, born out of a desire to reflect "the strong characteristics of God," would catapult itself into the hearts and repertoires of worshipers around the world. Steve admits songs like "God of Wonders" are rare for songwriters: "It's one of those things where a lot of us who write songs all the time know you'd write something like that every day if you could, but you just can't . . . it's just one of those moments."

For more than twenty years, California native Hindalong has made his creative mark on Christian music. He's a founding member, drummer/percussionist, and lyricist of The Choir, a band which forged new paths in Christian music's alternative and modern rock scenes across twelve albums. Hindalong has also produced other artists, including Common Children, Prayer Chain, and The Waiting. The Nashville resident's most indelible mark of late is his work with the City on a Hill series. City on a Hill—Songs of Worship and Praise, the original City series project, garnered Hindalong a Dove Award nomination for Producer of the Year in 2001. Away from the studio, Hindalong plays in the band at his local Episcopal church.

YOUR WORSHIP
ADVENTURE

STOP TO RECOGNIZE (AND REVEL IN) THE WONDERS OF HIS WORLD
AND HIS LOVE IN YOUR EVERY DAY. WHAT HAVE YOU SEEN OR
EXPERIENCED TODAY THAT MANIFESTS HIS GLORY?

REMEMBER

REMEMBER

"WHAT WE HAVE ONCE ENJOYED WE CAN NEVER LOSE.
ALL THAT WE LOVE DEEPLY BECOMES A PART OF US."

HELEN KELLER

We Speak to Nations
Israel Houghton

Hear the sound, the sound of the nations worshiping
Hear the sound of sons and daughters singing
Hear the sound, the sound of the nations calling
Hear the sound, sound of the fatherless crying
Who will go for us
Who will shout to the corners of the earth
That Christ is King?

We speak to nations be open
We speak to nations fall on your knees
We speak to nations
The kingdom is coming near to you
We speak to strongholds be broken
Powers of darkness you have to flee
We speak to nations
The kingdom is coming near to you
We speak to you
Be free, be free

ELEVEN

I CAN STILL REMEMBER THE FIRST TIME I KNEW I WANTED A MOMENT TO LAST FOREVER.

I was seven years old and standing in the back of a pickup truck as it rolled down a country road. The trees were so close to the road that as I stood with one hand holding a rail and the other flung out to the wind, the leaves brushed and whooshed across my hands, arms, and occasionally even splashed my face, while the truck bumped up and down the gravel road. I can still feel everything about that day—the way the wind went by, the way the sun flickered in and out and through the leaves, the way it felt when a flurry of leaves blew through my hair. I remember even saying it out loud: I wanted this moment to last forever . . . Thirty years later I remember the moment, but I'm not sure I can recall the passion of that moment—which, I suppose, is the part that I *really* wanted to carry with me into the rest of my life. The last thing I'd like to do right now is climb on the back of a truck and attempt to relive the stunt. But I really do hope to feel that feeling again. That moment when the world is perfect and rolling itself out at your feet. The moment you know you might trade a thousand other moments of your life for just to live this one again.

C. S. Lewis compares our lives and our memories to a ride on a train. We are constantly moving forward, taking in new worlds and scenes, but in fact we leave nothing behind.

No matter how many turns we take, hills we climb, stations we stop at, we still have with us everything we had when we first stepped

IT'S NOTHING MORE THAN A REMINDER OF THIS: NOTHING IS IRREDEEMABLE.

on board. It all comes with us through every day we live. Our memories, good and bad, are always a part of who we are and everything we will become. I suspect that the luckier you are in life and love, the more wishing-it-could-last-forever moments you have. But even for the rest of us who drag along timeworn memories we'd rather leave behind, there's still the hope that all we carry leads to something good. And maybe it's only because of the memories we carry that we can begin to dream what can be.

The good news is that anything we could possibly imagine is still ahead of us, and what we never imagined we'd ever live through never did, in fact, throw us off the train. We're still here, and along with us, every piece we've picked up to make us who we are.

Here's the silver lining. The baggage you wish you could toss? It's nothing more than a reminder of this: Nothing is irredeemable. Nothing. Every hurt can become a treasure, every ending a new beginning, every tear a burst of laughter. And finally, the only moment that really lasts forever is the one where we say yes—yes to God, to life, to memory. Yes, I will take whatever comes my way and let You make it whatever it needs to become.

Just imagine the possibilities.

YOUR WORSHIP ADVENTURE

HAVE YOU EVER HAD A MOMENT YOU WANTED TO LAST FOREVER?
TRY TO RECALL THE TIME AND PLACE AND RETELL THE STORY.
HOW ABOUT A MOMENT YOU'D LIKE TO TOSS OFF THE TRAIN?
WHICH ONE MEANS MORE TO YOU NOW?

DARE

DARE

"THE DREAM WAS ALWAYS RUNNING AHEAD OF ME.
TO CATCH UP, TO LIVE FOR A MOMENT
IN UNISON WITH IT, THAT WAS THE MIRACLE."

ANAÏS NIN

We All Bow Down
Lenny LeBlanc

*Princes and paupers, sons and daughters
Kneel at the throne of grace
Losers and winners, saints and sinners
One day will see His face*

*Summer and winter, the mountains and rivers
Whisper our Savior's name
Awesome and Holy, a friend to the lonely
Forever His love will reign*

He's the light of the world, and Lord of the Cross

*And we all bow down
Kings will surrender their crowns
And worship Jesus
Worship Jesus
Worship Jesus
For He is the love
Unfailing love
He is the Love of God*

TWELVE

WHEN DOROTHY AND HER TRIO OF MISFITS ENTER THE EMERALD CITY AND DISCOVER THAT THE WONDERFUL WIZARD OF OZ IS REALLY JUST . . .

. . . a well-placed microphone and some lights-and-mirrors chicanery, well, who wouldn't be heartbroken? Just when they thought they'd found everything they'd been looking for, the awful truth is revealed. "Pay no attention to the man behind the curtain," the man behind the wizard desperately calls into the microphone. Too late. His gig is up. Meanwhile, three road-worn travelers are left to deal with a bag full of washed up wishes.

Of course, the story doesn't end there. In

fact, everyone discovers that somehow down that yellow brick road, everything they needed was found in the journey and not in what ultimately became that disappointing destination. "Which of you," Jesus asks, "if his son asks for bread, will give him a stone?" It's ludicrous, He offers, to even think you cannot have anything you need, that you cannot get anything you dream of, when an ever-loving Father is the one you ask. No one was ever promised, however, that the gift would come wrapped exactly the way we expect. And sometimes we already have what we ask for; we just need the eyes to see it. Just ask the Scarecrow, the Tin Man, and the Lion—it didn't take a brain, a heart, or a whole lot of courage to see that they ended up getting way more than they bargained for.

"Life is what happens when you're busy making other plans," John Lennon wrote in one of his songs. Life is what happens even when we're out there looking for it. You can

---

THE ENCHANTMENT OF THE EVERYDAY IN HIS KINGDOM IS WORTH MORE THAN ANY EXOTIC DESTINATION YOU REACH FOR IN YOUR DREAMS.

---

get so consumed in the quest to find it that you might not even know when it knocks on your door. Jesus promised that an abundant life was not something to be experienced as a final goal, but something to be found in our daily trek. Even Dorothy, three clicks away from Kansas, had to figure out she was really home all along. "Somewhere over the rainbow" turned out to be right in her own backyard.

All that we ever hope to be is already inside us. And because of the wonderful things God does, discovering that is right in our sights. The enchantment of the everyday in His Kingdom is worth more than any exotic destination you reach for in your dreams. Let the storm take you away.

YOUR WORSHIP
ADVENTURE

While you've been busy "making other plans," try to discover
what God has already been doing in your life. Are there
things you have been asking for that you really already have?

JOURNAL

BELIEVE

"Now faith is being sure of what we hope for and certain of what we do not see."

Hebrews 11:1

Blessed Assurance

Fanny J. Crosby and Phoebe P. Knapp

Blessed assurance, Jesus is mine
O what a foretaste of glory divine
Heir of salvation, purchase of God
Born of His Spirit, washed in His blood

Perfect submission, all is at rest
I in my Savior am happy and blessed
Watching and waiting, looking above
Filled with His goodness, lost in His love

This is my story, this is my song
Praising my Savior all the day long
This is my story, this is my song
Praising my Savior all the day long

Perfect submission, perfect delight
Visions of rapture now burst on my sight
Angels descending bring from above
Echoes of mercy, whispers of love

THIRTEEN

"FAITH BEGINS," WRITES KIERKEGAARD, "PRECISELY WHERE THINKING LEAVES OFF."

Basically speaking, whatever you think can't happen, can. What's incomprehensible to the human mind is where something larger has to take over—something that doesn't begin with man, but with God. Maybe that's why, when Jesus grabbed the little kid running by and told His followers that unless you become like this, you'll never enter the kingdom of heaven—they had a bit of trouble catching His drift. After all, they'd gone through hell and high water following Him—and probably had a sneaking suspicion there was more to come.

How on earth could a runny-nosed kid have one up on them?

Well, for one thing, while the disciples

> ## I WORSHIP
> because I have to . . . Like breathing, it is essential to life. Without it we cannot fully communicate to our Creator. God made music, and He made it so we can appreciate the language of it. It is the "other" form of communication that goes beyond the mystical and should not be packaged to sell. Even though at times it is.
>
> —*Kevin Max; Artist, Songwriter, Poet*

spent the better part of their days asking Jesus questions, the children were content to just sit back and watch the show. They didn't need a scholar to explain the finer details of what was happening; they just accepted that everything He said and did (even though it was a little far from what they were used to) was pretty much the way things should be.

While the adults clutched their faith like ancient idols, clinging ferociously to what they had so none of it might seep through their fingers, the children grasped faith as easily as grabbing the hand of a friend standing next to them. They say that children should be seen and not heard, but Jesus Himself recommended listening. Maybe He knew that what we'd write off as foolish babbling really could hold the secrets of the Universe.

"Blessed are the pure in heart," He says, "for they shall see God." Not God as a reward in the sweet by and by, but God—here and now. That the pure in heart shall see God isn't a promise, it's a statement. The pure in heart already see God . . . everywhere. You can see Him in the beauty of the still night sky, in the sweetness of a dream realized, in the kindness of a stranger. If you know what you're looking for . . .

The poet Yeats prayed "that I may seem, though I die old, a foolish, passionate man." He probably saw that leaving this world with a child's eyes was the most he could hope for and the best he could ask. His prayer is as much a hope for living as an epitaph for leaving. No matter how bad things may seem, how dark the world spins, how sad each day spends itself out—it is the hope of the fools, the hope of the children and children at heart, that springs eternal. And to die foolish, holding on to a childlike grasp of the world, believing at once that everything that's ending is really just the beginning of the next adventure--this is where thinking leaves off and faith really begins.

YOUR WORSHIP ADVENTURE

WHERE DOES YOUR FAITH BEGIN? HOW MUCH OF WHAT YOU BELIEVE
DO YOU HAVE TO PROVE AND HOW MUCH DO YOU JUST TRUST,
EVEN WITHOUT HAVING PROOF?

i·JOURNAL

RUN

RUN

"LIKE MADNESS IS THE GLORY OF THIS LIFE."

SHAKESPEARE

All Hail the Pow'r of Jesus' Name
Edward Perronet and Oliver Holden

All hail the pow'r of Jesus' name
Let angels prostrate fall
Bring forth the royal diadem
And crown Him Lord of all
Bring forth the royal diadem
And crown Him Lord of all

Ye chosen seed of Israel's race
Ye ransomed from the fall
Hail Him who saves you by His grace
And crown Him Lord of all
Hail Him who saves you by His grace
And crown Him Lord of all

Let every kindred every tribe
On this terrestrial ball
To Him all majesty ascribe
And crown Him Lord of all
To Him all majesty ascribe
And crown Him Lord of all

MADNESS IS AN ALL-CONSUMING PASSION. AND IN THE HANDS OF A FIERY GOD, IT IS THE NEVER-ENDING POWER OF REDEMPTION.

Like the love-driven Don Quixote, with more heart than reason, He is the knight who will rise to any challenge in His quest to capture those He loves. One has the feeling He'd fence a thousand defenseless windmills just to win back the heart of one lost and lonely soul. To dream the impossible dream, indeed.

The poet Francis Thompson called this crazy, sacred pursuer "the Hound of Heaven" in his ode to the chase of his life. No matter how many "labyrinth ways" he zigged or zagged, trying to flee that holy, constant hunter, He was unshakable. And the more the poet raced to escape from the dogged pursuit, the louder he heard above him the pounding feet, continuing the mad dash.

"I fled Him . . . and in the mist of tears I hid from Him, and under running laughter." "It becomes obvious we are dealing with a maniac," says Annie Dillard of her own dealings with this God. He is a reckless, raging power of the universe—willingly trapped inside His own seemingly reasonless desire to capture and redeem every life back to Himself. And He'll go to any length to do it.

Pure madness is what any sane observer might call it. But what else would explain His ways? A Messiah who arrives not to conquer kings, but hearts. A ruler who comes to break all the rules and let everyone in. A master of singular power who lives as a servant to all. A Christ to be sought who instead pursues, even the ones who run away.

WHEN THE WORLD IS AT YOUR FEET, YOU DON'T NEED TO RACE AFTER IT. BUT LOVE HAS AN INCREDIBLE WAY OF DOING CRAZY THINGS.

The chase is mad. No other god the world has ever created would have dreamed of it. When you hold the universe in your hands, you don't have to go chasing down anything else. When the world is at your feet, you don't need to race after it. But love has an incredible way of doing crazy things. A whole lot of heart and just a little bit of madness can go a long way toward saving the world. Redemption really does draw nigh every time He picks up His sword and heads out on that knightly quest for your heart.

Some people think it's crazy to dream the impossible dream, to fight the unbeatable foe, to run where the brave dare not go. Not this Savior. Even the chance of netting just one heart seemed worth it all to Him.

In fact, He died trying.

YOUR WORSHIP ADVENTURE

HAVE YOU EVER TRIED TO RUN AWAY FROM GOD?
OR AT LEAST RUN AWAY FROM SOMETHING HE WAS TRYING TO SHOW
YOU? STOP AND REMEMBER THE STORY OF YOUR PURSUIT AND
HOW YOU WERE FINALLY "CAPTURED."

JOURNAL

CELEBRATE

"BUT BY THE GRACE OF GOD I AM WHAT I AM,
AND HIS GRACE TO ME WAS NOT WITHOUT EFFECT."

———————

I CORINTHIANS 15:10

Grace Alone
Scott Wesley Brown and Jeff Nelson

Every promise we can make
Every prayer and step of faith
Every difference we will make
Is only by His grace

Every mountain we will climb
Every ray of hope we shine
Every blessing left behind
Is only by His grace

Every loving word we say
Every tear we wipe away
Every sorrow turned to praise
Is only by His grace

Grace alone which God supplies
Strength unknown He will provide
Christ in us our cornerstone
We will go forth in grace alone

FIFTEEN

I'M NOT A BIG FAN OF MOST BUMPER STICKERS. THE FACT THAT YOUR MOTHER-IN-LAW IS IN THE TRUNK OR THAT YOUR OTHER CAR IS A PORSCHE WAS ONLY FUNNY THE FIRST FOUR OR FIVE TIMES.

Of course, it's also good to know that no matter how many times you turn left without signaling, "You're not perfect, just forgiven." And even though I never thought to blame you for anything, I can't, because you voted for whoever lost.

Then I saw it. A simple little white sticker tacked on the back of a beat-up old Datsun with two little words shining over the rust:

GRACE HAPPENS. I certainly knew that the other thing that bumper stickers usually say happens happens, but this one meant so much more. Yes. Grace does happen. All the time. Everywhere I and that little Datsun go. Good stuff can hit us as randomly as the bad stuff. It's just that the good stuff never makes the front page.

A plane goes down and the newscaster, without emotion, can read the number of people who won't go home again. People with bombs bigger than their ideas randomly pick a building and take it and all the people in it away in one awful blast. And innocents die, and love ends, and life remains eternally unfair. And we wonder, for the millionth time, why bad things have to happen, even to strangers— because we know it just as easily could be us.

But grace tiptoes along more silently and invisibly than those clanging chimes of doom. The kindness of a stranger streaks its light across our room; mercy is in the middle of the heart of someone whose forgiveness we beg; another plane bursts through the air, defies all laws of ground and gravity, and brings home the one we love most. And when that good happens, we forget to ask why. The One we easily blame and whine to for all the bad is still the Giver of all good things who never gives up trying to show us the miracle of just being alive.

"Miracles," wrote Willa Cather, "seem to me to rest not so much upon faces or voices or healing power coming suddenly near to us from afar off, but upon our perceptions being made finer, so that for a moment our eyes can see and our ears can hear what is there about us always."

There's real grace for you—God opening our ears enough to hear the music of life buzzing around us and widening our eyes to the ever-present, extravagant light of His love. And this isn't showtime, this is His everyday fare. A God that even heaven couldn't hold doesn't need a televised miracle service in order to show up. His grace happens everywhere—even in the middle of a traffic jam that has you left with nothing to do but read every bumper that surrounds you. Remember to look for Him while you're there. And don't forget to honk if you love it.

WHAT'S AMAZING ABOUT THE GRACE IN YOUR LIFE? TRY TO REMEMBER
AND RECOUNT A TIME WHEN THE GRACE OF GOD EXPLODED IN YOUR
LIFE—WHEN YOU REALLY KNEW IT WAS "A MESSAGE FROM GOD."

DAY SIXTEEN

WORSHIP

"HE HAS SHOWED YOU, O MAN, WHAT IS GOOD.
AND WHAT DOES THE LORD REQUIRE OF YOU?
TO ACT JUSTLY AND TO LOVE MERCY AND TO
WALK HUMBLY WITH YOUR GOD."

MICAH 6:8

Be Unto Your Name

Lynn Deshazo and Gary Sadler

We are a moment, You are forever
Lord of the ages, God before time
We are a vapor, You are eternal
Love everlasting, reigning on high

Holy holy Lord God Almighty
Worth is the Lamb who was slain
Highest praises, honor and glory
Be unto Your name
Be unto Your name

We are the broken, You are the healer
Jesus, Redeemer, mighty to save
You are the love song we'll sing forever
Bowing before You, blessing Your name

Be Unto Your Name

WORDS FROM THE SONGWRITER
GARY SADLER

WE ARE A MOMENT, YOU ARE FOREVER . . .

WE ARE A MOMENT . . . *"Happy birthday to you."*
Singing or hearing this song has the power to carry me
back into my distant memories (as do certain other
sounds, fragrances, images, and temperatures). Back to the
who and where and how of then. It's only by reference
of time that we find a conduit, a passageway, between
then and now.

Once upon a time I was a two-year-old, with all of
these years I've lived since still ahead of me. Now I have
a grandson who is two with most of his great life laid out
there in front of him. Before him are the choices, common
to all and yet unique to him, that will draw his own shape
and paint his own colors (whether bold or subdued, his
very soul's expression) on the wonderful mystery canvas

of his life. And given enough time, it will become unde-
niably clear to him that these seconds that become hours,
and hours that become years, pass much more quickly
than he thought possible. The same could be said for
all of us.

To make matters worse (so it would seem), we can
neither hold the days past nor touch the days yet to come.
We are captive, kept within the boundaries of time.
All we have is now, this very moment.

Perhaps like me, you have come to view your entire
existence as lasting but an instant, as though we were
mere vapor. And so it is.

Or is it?

You are forever . . . The God who created us
and the days in which we live exists outside of the realm
of time, unbound by the intervals of seasons or eons.
And we are formed in His image . . . made to know and

partake in what is described best not only by terms of length, but kind of life. His life, like His love, is without

---

TO MAKE MATTERS WORSE (SO IT WOULD SEEM), WE CAN NEITHER HOLD THE DAYS PAST NOR TOUCH THE DAYS YET TO COME. WE ARE CAPTIVE, KEPT WITHIN THE BOUNDARIES OF TIME.

---

dimension. God is the reality we must come face to face with, not in the days behind or in the days ahead, but in the present; to worship Him in the only moment within our grasp . . . what we call "now."

It is now, and always now—in these moments

defined by measures of time—that our hearts meet
His to share the gifts of His life and join in the eternal
stream of worship, giving highest praises, honor, and
glory to His name. Our journey here is brief, but the

Gary Sadler is a songwriter/musician/producer who has written many songs performed by artists as varied as Sonicflood, Kim Hill, Phillips, Craig & Dean, Lenny LeBlanc, and Sarah Sadler (yes, one of two very talented daughters). Gary and his wife, Debra, live in Franklin, TN.

"Be Unto Your Name" was written by Lynn DeShazo and Gary Sadler in 1996. Gary says, "We were at my house talking all around the topic of the brevity of life, and the lines came 'We are a moment' . . . and so on. We wrote the first verse and came to the chorus, realizing all we could sing was 'Holy,' and we knew we had tapped into something every heart was longing to say."

EVERY DAY IS A GIFT FROM GOD, AND WE ARE ASKED TO USE IT WELL
AS A GIFT BACK TO HIM. WHAT CAN YOU DO TODAY THAT IS
AN INVESTMENT IN FOREVER?

i · JOURNAL

FOLLOW

DAY SEVENTEEN

FOLLOW

"FOR I KNOW THE PLANS I HAVE FOR YOU,
DECLARES THE LORD, PLANS TO PROSPER
YOU AND NOT TO HARM YOU, PLANS TO GIVE
YOU HOPE AND A FUTURE."

JEREMIAH 29:11

Every Move I Make
David Ruis

Every move I make, I make in You
You make me move, Jesus
Every breath I take, I breathe in You
Every step I take, I take in You
You are my way, Jesus
Every breath I take, I breathe in You

Waves of mercy, waves of grace
Everywhere I look I see Your face
Your love has captured me,
O my God
This love how can it be

SEVENTEEN

BACK IN THE '80S A POPULAR ROCK BAND TOOK SOME ANCIENT WORDS OF LITURGY AND TURNED THEM INTO A RADIO HIT.

The song "Kyrie Eleison" had millions crying out the timeless prayer of "Lord, have mercy" with a decidedly modern bent. The band's version went further with the plaintive line, "Kyrie Eleison, where I'm going will You follow?" It was a beautiful twist on an old idea. Instead of "Lord, have mercy, tell me where to go," the song merely asked for mercy and God's companionship down whatever road ended up being traveled. God, it is assumed, doesn't need to wind us up and set us on a path; He merely asks that we invite Him on our own journey. What a celebration of the gift of freedom He does give us all. He promises to

> ### I WORSHIP
> because God is worthy and that is the only reason we need. But in the last few years there are some things I have been thinking. God uses worship to prepare our hearts to receive ministry, to prepare us to minister to others, and I believe that many battles are won in the spiritual realm when we worship. People who don't know God are drawn to Him.
>
> *—Twila Paris; Artist and Songwriter*

lead, but He never shoves. You and I are free to walk whatever road our hearts desire.

There's the paradox. We're the followers

of a leader who lets us choose our own way. For better or for worse. I suspect we all have the knack for usually choosing the worst.

I ONCE THOUGHT THAT GOD PLUNKING US DOWN IN THE MIDDLE OF NOWHERE WITH ONLY OUR OWN DEVICES TO FIGURE OUT THE WAY AROUND WAS AN UNUSUALLY CRUEL MOVE.

I once thought that God plunking us down in the middle of nowhere with only our own devices to figure out the way around was an unusually cruel move. When you're God, couldn't You just make things a little more obvious? I reasoned. I was hitting far too many potholes to make this a loving option. I knew all about joy being in the journey, but sometimes a little less joy and a little more direction would be nice. Or like the refrigerator magnet philosopher admonishes, "Lead, follow, or get out of the way." God, it appears, doesn't listen to fridge magnets. In fact, my hunch is He'll lead if you want Him to, follow along if you ask, or get right out of the way for as long as you decide to keep it that way. One wonders where He gets the patience for all of it.

But as for this road, this day, I am begging Him to follow. Lord, have mercy. And somehow beside me, I think I hear the whisper, "Go ahead, check it out . . . I'm right behind you. All the way. Even to the ends of the earth."

Have you ever asked God to lead, follow, or get out of the way?
Try to recall the instances where God has done one or
all three in any of the circumstances of your life.

_____

_____

_____

_____

_____

_____

_____

_____

_____

_____

_____

_____

_____

_____

_____

_____

_____

_____

_____

_____

DAY EIGHTEEN
GRASP

"THEN JESUS TOLD HIM, 'BECAUSE YOU HAVE SEEN ME, YOU HAVE BELIEVED; BLESSED ARE THOSE WHO HAVE NOT SEEN AND YET HAVE BELIEVED.'"

JOHN 20:29

You're Worthy of My Praise
David Ruis

I will worship with all of my heart
I will praise You with all of my strength
I will seek You all of my days
I will follow all of Your ways

I will give You all my worship
I will give You all my praise
You alone I long to worship
You alone are worthy of my praise

I'm gonna bow down and hail You as King
I will serve You, I'll give You everything
I will lift up my eyes to Your throne
I will trust You, trust You alone

EIGHTEEN

BELIEF IN
THE INFINITE
UNFATHOMABLE-NESS
OF GOD IS THE
ONLY THING THAT
KEEPS ME SANE.

Or as sane as I can currently possibly be. I understand how men have gone mad over the centuries trying to figure it out. But as Zorba declared in all his Greek glory, a man must have a little madness or else he'll never dare to cut the rope and be free.

God is eternally too big to understand. God is too big to ever wrap our arms around. You'll go crazy before you could ever begin to take Him all in. But I will tenaciously cling to any piece of Him I can. Whatever He will let me see, touch, hear, or feel—that I can keep and trust and know. Know that, mysteriously, He somehow still lets all of Himself reside in whatever piece of Himself I hold, even as all

> ### I WORSHIP
> not by something I do, as much as something that happens to me when a few elements are in place. Those elements, simply put, are (1) a time when my soul is receptive and searching for Him; (2) a context in which there aren't a lot of distractions from the here-and-now; and (3) a sign of Himself through a song, something said in a sermon, or a memory of God in my past experience that comes to mind. And then worship occurs.
>
> *—John Townsend, Author*

the rest of it spills and swirls outside my grasp.

"Lord, I believe; help my unbelief," may very well be one of the most honest prayers the Bible has recounted for us. "You don't even have to explain it, God," the asker seems to say, "just let me believe. No matter how mad it sounds." It is entirely possible, he

---

GOD NEVER ASKED US TO FIGURE HIM OUT; HE ONLY ASKED US TO BELIEVE.

---

supposes, to believe even if you can't believe it. Writer Frederick Buechner imagines that if theology is what we call the study of God, perhaps dung beetles may study man and call it humanology. "If so," he adds, "we would probably be more touched and amused than irritated. One hopes that God feels likewise."

I have to believe He does.

What parent would love a child less for not being able to articulate how the car runs, or where the rain comes from, or why the light flickers? It's impossible. What father would turn away the son who just didn't understand how loved he was? God never asked us to figure Him out; He only asked us to believe. As unbelievable as it sounds or tastes or feels, I think there must be a magic to this whole strange story that we will never, ever know until the day it probably won't matter anymore. There's a reason He's beyond reason. You'd be crazy to try and explain it.

IF YOU COULD ASK GOD TO FULLY EXPLAIN JUST ONE THING,
WHAT WOULD YOUR QUESTION BE?

i-JOURNAL

BEGIN

BEGIN

> "FOR ALL THAT HAS BEEN, THANKS.
> FOR ALL THAT SHALL BE, YES."

DAG HAMMARSKJÖLD

That's Why We Praise Him
Tommy Walker

He came to live, live a perfect life
He came to be the Living Word, our light
He came to die so we'd be reconciled
He came to rise, to show His pow'r and might

That's why we praise Him, that's why we sing
That's why we offer Him our everything
That's why we bow down and worship this King
'Cause He gave IIis everything
'Cause He gave His everything

He came to live, live again in us
He came to be our conquering King and Friend
He came to heal and show the lost ones His love
He came to go prepare a place for us

NINETEEN

THERE WAS A TIME—I MUST HAVE BEEN FIVE OR SIX YEARS OLD—WHEN IT DAWNED ON ME THAT IF PEOPLE HAD A BEGINNING, THEN SOMEHOW, TOO, GOD MUST HAVE HAD A BEGINNING.

I chose the moment for my dramatic question, and asked my busied mother when God was born. She deftly sent me to my grandfather, who happened to be strolling around the yard at the time.

I dutifully, and with great purpose, stalked him down and together we sat on a bench in the shade at the side of the house. "Mom says you know when God was born," I informed him. "So when was it?"

He was nonplussed. He didn't hesitate. He didn't stammer. He didn't even look up and think with that movie-moment pause.

> ### I WORSHIP
> even when I don't feel like it because God inhabits the praises of his people. So when we worship or when we choose to offer a sacrifice of praise, God meets us and He realigns our priorities. He brings healing, and I find quickly that because of God's response to my worship, I do feel like worshiping.
>
> —*Twila Paris; Artist and Songwriter*

"God was never born," he said. "He just always is." That was it. I didn't even have a follow-up question. My grandfather was so certain that I bought into that certainty even before I bought into the truth of what he said. God just always is.

I have yet to understand this—even though I do believe it. Eternity, time, infinity . . . it's all just a little too much to take in. How

---

THE ONE WHO NEVER HAD A BEGINNING BEGAN A NEW WORLD THAT DAY.

---

can anything be everlasting when all we ever know on this side of it all is that nothing lasts forever? As a child I almost understood forever. After all, it seemed like anything you wanted to happen did take that long. As an adult, I too readily know that forever ends too soon and that a goodbye always comes too quickly after a first hello. God Himself was even willing to enter our own understanding of time, landing smack-dab in the middle of nowhere for a chance to show us the way. Infinite became finite in one angel-strewn little town. And for one brief, shining moment, God was born—and chose to live among us for awhile.

The One who never had a beginning began a new world that day. His birth in that starlit manger set off the promise that continues to be born in us again every new day. There are no more old souls. No more hopeless causes. And for every tear-drenched goodbye, there is the promise of a glorious hello. Every ending is really the beginning. You'd of had to been born yesterday not to see it.

YOUR WORSHIP
ADVENTURE

WHY DO YOU PRAISE HIM? COULD YOU STILL, EVEN IN YOUR DARKEST
HOURS? WHAT DO YOU THANK HIM FOR IN YOUR LIFE,
NO MATTER WHAT YOU MAY BE GOING THROUGH?

JOURNAL

RETURN

RETURN

"...BUT WHILE HE WAS STILL A LONG WAY OFF,
HIS FATHER SAW HIM AND WAS FILLED WITH
COMPASSION FOR HIM; HE RAN TO HIS SON,
THREW HIS ARMS AROUND HIM AND KISSED HIM."

LUKE 15:20

Sing for Joy
Lamont Hiebert

If we call to Him He will answer us
If we run to Him He will run to us
If we lift our hands He will lift us up
Come now, praise His name
All you saints of God

Sing for joy to God our strength
Sing for joy to God our strength

Draw near to Him, He is here with us
Give Him your love, He's in love with us
He will heal our hearts, He will cleanse our hands
If we rend our hearts He will heal our land

THOMAS WOLFE MAY HAVE THOUGHT HE HAD IT RIGHT WHEN HE SAID, "YOU CAN'T GO HOME AGAIN"— BUT THEN HE'D HAVE TO ARGUE WITH MY MOTHER. Yours too, probably. Her defiance of his proclamation is the only thing that ever got me out of the house. "You can always come back" was the only security I needed to take that first bold step outside. I always knew that no matter where I went or what I did, I *could* always come home again.

In the parable of the prodigal son, Jesus introduces us to a pigheaded boy who didn't care much whether he could come home again or not. His fortune was out there to be found, and the further and faster he got away from his provincial life, the happier he knew he'd be. But as he later discovered—taking him a little longer than most of us—you usually leave a lot more than just an empty bedroom and some outdated clothes behind. When you're really lucky (and he was, even before he knew it), you also leave behind someone who loves you and sits waiting for the day you return. Prodigal or not.

The son in this story eventually figured out that at least he could return to a warm bed if nothing else. After his romp on the wild side he couldn't even imagine being extended any more grace than that. The surprise, of course, was that he had not only a warm bed waiting, but everything else his little heart desired.

You really can almost see that picture of that world-weary son tramping back down the road home . . . and the father ready to

---

THE FATHER KNEW THAT NOTHING WAS RIGHT UNTIL THAT ONE PRECIOUS SOUL WAS BACK IN HIS SIGHT.

---

meet him more than halfway. The father who never stopped hoping. Never stopped waiting. The father who knew that nothing was right until that one precious soul was back in his sight.

A songwriter described the story as "when God ran." The prodigal son marveled at the miracle of this love. "It was the only time I ever saw Him run, when He ran to me." There is nowhere you can go and no distance you can travel that can take you too far away from home—and the One there waiting for you.

No matter how many roads you go down, how many miles you clock, or how far you roam, back home a loving Father is waiting for the day you return. And no matter how long it's been, know that on that day you do come home, there is a light to guide your way. Because Someone always leaves the porch light on.

YOUR WORSHIP
ADVENTURE

HOME MEANS COMFORT. WHERE ARE YOU MOST COMFORTABLE?
IS IT THE PLACE, OR THE PEOPLE IN IT, THAT GIVES YOU THAT SECURITY?

TRUST

TRUST

"Trust in the Lord with all your heart and lean not on your own understanding; in all your ways acknowledge him, and he will make your paths straight."

PROVERBS 3:5-6

What a Friend I've Found

Martin Smith

*What a friend I've found
Closer than a brother
I have felt Your touch
More intimate than lovers*

Jesus, Jesus, Jesus, friend forever

*What a hope I've found
More faithful than a mother
It would break my heart
To ever lose each other*

Jesus, Jesus, Jesus, friend forever

*Lord, I am so in love with You
And Lord, I stand to proclaim Your truth
Jesus, You're my friend forever*

TWENTY-ONE

IN HER BOOK *TRAVELING MERCIES*, WRITER ANNE LAMOTT RECOUNTS THAT IRONIC TALE OF THE SAD DRUNK POURING OUT HIS WOES TO A PATIENT BARTENDER IN THE COLD NORTH OF ALASKA. Seems the teller of the tale, while piloting his plane through the darkness, took an unfortunate plunge into the winter wilderness, and though he survived the fall, he sat stranded for days in the cold of his wreckage. He begged. He pleaded. He prayed for God to help him out of his misery. But it was to no avail. His faith was gone. God never listened. God never came. "But you're here," the bartender counters. "You were saved." "Yeah," the drunk grouses back, "only because an Eskimo finally came and found me."

I've let a hundred Eskimos come and find me and still I'll shake my fists in the air. My favorite conversations with God all begin with "Why?" and "Where are You?" And I spend so much time asking, I forget to look for the answers that I'm sure are raining down on my head at every turn.

Jesus probably came in the most distressing disguise of history: the king of the world as a penniless peasant, the God of the ages as the scourge of His time. You gotta believe He loves a great scheme. And from the moment He set foot on earth, He made it clear He's going to do whatever it takes to get it through our heads and our hearts: He's promised us the pleasure of His presence through a hundred other eyes, arms, feet, rocks, birds, songs, machines, fires, mountains, kings, Eskimos, and wild-eyed three-year-olds. He even

JESUS PROBABLY CAME IN THE MOST DISTRESSING DISGUISE OF HISTORY: THE KING OF THE WORLD AS A PENNILESS PEASANT.

promised that we can have a part in the masquerade. God can use any thing He wants to send His message home. And sometimes He's brave enough to use us.

He's the cosmic micromanager. You're lonely and looking for a way out? Watch out for the new neighbor who's been busy praying for someone to help him with that fence. You know God's going to smack those two together. Need a boost for the blues? Here comes the harried mother praying for an emergency babysitter. (It's pretty hard to keep moping with that gurgling little bundle in your arms.) Another slam-dunk. Or like the joke goes, "I asked God for patience, and boy, did He give it to me!" Careful what you ask for . . . you know you're going to end up playing His game. Learn to expect the unexpected. And when you're numb from praying without ceasing about whatever you so desperately need, remember to watch for more than just those angels of rescue. And for heaven's sake, trust that *He* sent the Eskimo.

YOUR WORSHIP
ADVENTURE

TRY TO RECALL YOUR OWN "ESKIMO" EXPERIENCE.
DO YOU REMEMBER A TIME WHEN GOD ANSWERED YOUR PRAYER
IN THE MOST UNLIKELY AND UNEXPECTED WAY?

INVITE

INVITE

"MY EYES STAY OPEN THROUGH THE WATCHES
OF THE NIGHT, THAT I MAY
MEDITATE ON YOUR PROMISES."

PSALM 119:148

Open the Eyes of My Heart
Paul Baloche

Open the eyes of my heart, Lord
Open the eyes of my heart
I want to see You, I want to see You
Open the eyes of my heart, Lord
Open the eyes of my heart
I want to see You, I want to see You

To see You high and lifted up
Shining in the light of Your glory
Pour out Your pow'r and love
As we sing holy, holy, holy

Holy, holy, holy
Holy, holy, holy
Holy, holy, holy
I want to see You

OPEN THE EYES OF MY HEART

WORDS FROM THE SONGWRITER

PAUL BALOCHE

I pray also that the eyes of your heart may be enlightened in order that you may know the hope to which he has called you, the riches of his glorious inheritance in the saints, and his incomparably great power for us who believe" (Ephesians 1:18-19).

When we contemplate Scripture, God's very personal message to us, it moves our hearts toward Him—sometimes it even inspires a song! It enables us to look up and see with spiritual eyes instead of focusing on ourselves and our earthly problems. It corrects our perspective.

"Therefore we do not lose heart. Though outwardly we are wasting away, yet inwardly we are being renewed day by day. For our light and momentary troubles are achieving for us an eternal glory that far outweighs them all. So we fix our eyes not on what is seen, but on what is unseen. For what is seen is temporary, but what is unseen is eternal" (2 Corinthians 4:16).

I encourage you, as you go through your daily routine, to keep a portion of Scripture—whether it's what you've read, heard from a pastor, discussed with a friend, or heard in a song—in your thoughts. Put it down on a Post-It note on your car dashboard or on the mirror in your bathroom or on the refrigerator door. Remind yourself of it regularly. What does it really mean? How can you apply it to your life? Pray that the Lord will enlighten you and bring appropriate verses to mind as you need them.

Not only do we want our eyes open to see God's truth in Scripture and in the world, but as this prayerful song says, we want to see God for who He is and understand Him as fully as we can with all of our *earthly trappings and limitations. We long "to see You high and lifted up, shining in the light of Your glory." We humbly ask, "Pour out Your pow'r and love, as we*

NOT ONLY DO WE WANT OUR
EYES OPEN TO SEE GOD'S
TRUTH . . . WE WANT TO SEE
GOD FOR WHO HE IS
AND UNDERSTAND HIM
AS FULLY AS WE CAN WITH
ALL OF OUR EARTHLY
TRAPPINGS AND LIMITATIONS.

---

sing holy, holy, holy." If we really try to wrap our minds around the concepts of God's holiness, awesome power, and perfect love, we must fall to our knees, bowed down in humility—bowled over by gratitude and amazement

*at the thought of this Person wanting us to know Him
and have fellowship with Him!*

Open the eyes of my heart, Lord. I want to see You.

"There was no real plan or struggle with lyrics or melody when I wrote this song," Paul Baloche says. "I was just playing guitar during a ministry time at my church and thinking about Ephesians 1:18-19. I began to prayerfully sing out to Him, 'Open the eyes of my heart, Lord, open the eyes of my heart,' over and over again, and the whole song pretty much rolled off my tongue. It really is a simple song that reflected the sincere prayer of my heart."

New Jersey native Paul Baloche grew up Catholic, so he always knew about God, but as a young adult he began a personal relationship with Jesus that changed the trajectory of his life. A music lover from a young age, Paul's natural musical talent, combined with his growing passion for God, developed into a thriving worship ministry. An integral part of Integrity Music's Hosanna Series, he has written more than 120 songs, including "Revival Fire Fall," "Sing Out," and "Open the Eyes of My Heart." In 2002, "Above All," a song he co-wrote with Lenny LeBlanc, won a Dove Award for Song of the Year. Paul and his wife, Rita—a great songwriter in her own right—live in Lindale, Texas.

ONE DAY WE WILL LITERALLY SEE HIM IN ALL OF HIS GLORY AND LIVE
IN HIS PRESENCE. IN THE MEANTIME, THINK OF ALL THE MANY WAYS
YOU CAN AND DO SEE HIM IN YOUR EVERYDAY LIFE. WHAT ARE THE
WORDS OF YOUR OWN PRAYER TO HIM TO LET YOU SEE MORE?

JOURNAL

LOVE

LOVE

"PLACE ME LIKE A SEAL OVER YOUR HEART,

LIKE A SEAL ON YOUR ARM;

FOR LOVE IS AS STRONG AS DEATH."

SONG OF SOLOMON 8:6

Redeemer Savior Friend
Darrell Evans and Chris Springer

I know You had me on Your mind
When You climbed up on that hill
For You saw me with eternal eyes
While I was yet in sin
Redeemer Savior Friend

Redeemer
Redeem my heart again
Savior, come and shelter me from sin
You're familiar with my weakness
Devoted to the end
Redeemer Savior Friend

So the grace You've poured upon my life
Will return to You in praise
And I'll gladly lay down all my crowns
For the name by which I'm saved
For the name by which I'm saved

ASIDE FROM THE ROMANCE OF A FEW HEROIC DYING SCENES SERVED UP ON HOLLYWOOD SCREENS, DEATH IS AN UGLY VISITOR.

It arrives without warning, comes coldly and silently, and buries more hearts than the one it came to steal. It is not hard to accept, therefore, the general rule of the living that says, basically, death is something to be avoided at all costs. But, as usual, exceptions to the rule make for the better story.

In *A Tale of Two Cities*, Carton, the hero, discovers—not too late—that love of another transcends the love of life. "It is a far, far better thing that I do, than I have ever done," he decides, and lets go of living so the one he loves can live. It is a rare thing when a man dies for one who loves him back; it is extraordinary when a man dies for someone he doesn't even know. It is a miracle when a man who owns all of heaven and earth dies for someone who doesn't even care that He did.

If all the world really is a stage, then surely the greatest scene ever played out upon it began when that hero declared, "It is finished." When the music slowed to a dreary dirge and the dazed players took down the stilled Godman to carry Him away, there began the drama that gave the kiss of death to a dying world and the breath of life to the new world beginning. "God seems to me to be an artist . . ." wrote Malcolm Muggeridge. "He has created the drama, and the parts of the play that are wicked and dreadful may be necessary to the whole creation in a way we can't understand."

Surely the players and the lovers and the villains who watched the play unfold that day saw only the awful darkness of both their sky and their souls as the man bound to the tree

THE DREAM MAY HAVE TO DIE
BEFORE IT CAN REALLY LIVE.
EVIL MAY PREVAIL BEFORE
THE GOOD CAN SAVE THE DAY.

in love came down broken and cold. Even the ones who thought Him a chump for bowing to so ugly a death for a few radical notions couldn't see the bigger story enveloping their little stage. Even the ones who loved Him and felt their hearts tear with His couldn't see the brighter light waiting behind the curtain. Yet.

"There is evil cast around us," sings songwriter David Wilcox, "but it's love that wrote the play." In great art, as in real life, there must always be rescue. Salvation, no matter how hidden, is at the core of any painting, any play, any song, any heart that dares attempt revelation of the great secret of life. The script reads: "I am the resurrection and the life, says the Lord." When love writes the story, the hero may have to battle the darkness before he can ride off into the sunset. The dream may have to die before it can really live. Evil may prevail before the good can save the day. But when the curtain finally falls, love will still be King, truth will still be triumphant, and death shall have no dominion.

THE BIBLE TALKS ABOUT A "NO GREATER LOVE" THAN THE ONE THAT
WILL LAY ITS LIFE DOWN FOR SOMEONE ELSE.
WRITE ABOUT THOSE LOVES IN YOUR OWN LIFE.

PERSEVERE

PERSEVERE

"COME, LET US RETURN TO THE LORD. HE HAS TORN
US TO PIECES BUT HE WILL HEAL US; HE HAS
INJURED US BUT HE WILL BIND UP OUR WOUNDS."

HOSEA 6:1

Trading My Sorrows
Darrell Evans

I'm trading my sorrows
I'm trading my shame
I'm laying them down
For the joy of the Lord.
I'm trading my sickness
I'm trading my pain
I'm laying them down
For the joy of the Lord

I am pressed but not crushed
Persecuted not abandoned
Struck down but not destroyed
I am blessed beyond the curse
For His promise will endure
That His joy's gonna be my strength
Though the sorrow may last for the night
His joy comes with the morning

"WHATEVER DOESN'T KILL YOU WILL MAKE YOU STRONGER" IS REALLY JUST ONE OF THOSE NICE WAYS OF SAYING THAT LIFE CAN BE A HUGE PAIN.

And a pain that might not even be worth it, at that. If the hard times don't get you down enough, worrying about them sure will. Life becomes nothing more than the neurotic waiting for that one thing that finally will get you.

Or if you take the more traditional approach, you can look at suffering and the "bad stuff" as nothing more than a great procession of lessons to make us better people. A noble obligation, to be sure, but not one that any would welcome with great joy. Job may have become a hero for the ages, but for all his learning he still had to lose his children, his home, his heart. Expensive education.

As for me, I don't want it. Suffering, that is. I don't want to have to spend hours running from it. And if it did catch up to me, I wouldn't care to take any lessons from it. If the rules mean I have to go through hell to learn something, I'd rather just read about it in a book. Unfortunately, yet again, I am not in charge here.

"God whispers to us in our pleasures, speaks in our conscience, but shouts in our pains," says C. S. Lewis, and that perhaps is more a reflection of our human character than it is of God's best plan for reaching His creations. If we'd listen to His whisper when everything was rosy, it wouldn't take a mega-phone of pain to get our attention. But why and how He chooses even to speak to us in the first place still remains a mystery. And how pain could be His calling card—a greater one still.

It is a less radical approach, but accepting the mystery of suffering seems to be the only real way out, or through. If you try to explain it, you end up looking like the lovable mutt trying to catch his tail as he haplessly circles the yard. Explain something like the Holocaust? Who could? Did it make anyone strong? If it did, I can't imagine that it was worth the price. On the other hand, if you somehow summon the unimaginable strength to actually welcome suffering, you're already in a place well beyond our day-to-day grind. I think it is only His maddest prophets and surreal-ly real saints that He's sprinkled sparingly on the planet who possess this rare gift.

To those of us caught in the middle of both, we can only, finally, look to Christ. "Surely he bore our sorrows," writes Isaiah, and surely He did see suffering from both its sides. As a man He walked and wept with every broken heart that met His gaze, and as Messiah, He himself became what we were so that we could somehow find a way through the mire. We crushed Him with our own evil, and instead of killing us for it, He made us stronger. We killed Him and He made us stronger. God works in mysterious ways.

YOUR WORSHIP ADVENTURE

THINK OF A TIME OR EVENT IN YOUR LIFE WHEN YOU NEVER THOUGHT YOU'D MAKE IT THROUGH. LOOKING BACK ON THE STORY NOW, TRY TO FIND THE FINGERPRINTS OF GOD THROUGH THAT STORY—WHERE HE LED YOU THROUGH EVEN IF YOU NEVER SAW IT AT THE TIME.

JOURNAL

IMAGINE

IMAGINE

"THE EARTH IS THE LORD'S,
AND EVERYTHING IN IT."

1 CORINTHIANS 10:26

Awesome God
Paul Garcia and Tim Johnson

You're my strength and You're my salvation
I will put my trust in You
My heart sings, in You my soul rejoices
In this song of praise to You

You are the awesome God
You are the great I AM
The only Living Word, Wonderful Counselor
Awesome God

You are the awesome God
You are the first and last
The only Living Word
Age to age still the same
Awesome God

TWENTY-FIVE

I NO LONGER
WISHED FOR A
BETTER WORLD
BECAUSE I WAS
THINKING OF THE
WHOLE OF
CREATION . . .

. . . and in
the light of
this clearer
discernment,
I have come to
see that, though the higher things are better
than the lower, the sum of all creation is better
than the higher things alone. I think
Augustine had it right when he decided that
life was hard and God was good, but that
either option without the other just didn't
have the right ring to it.

The merger of the sacred and the profane
has always been a fascinating dilemma. How

can one exist without destroying, or at the very least diminishing, the other? I don't know, but this I do know: It is the magnificent contradiction that gives life and color to everything we know and everything we don't want to know. How can we believe God is everywhere and yet presume to know what levels He won't stoop to for us to find Him there? How do we ever dare to assert our claim to name a place that God won't go, a vessel God won't use, a cry that He won't listen to?

"If I make my bed in hell," David marvels, "even there you are with me." Even there God will enter to prove the lengths of His love. He is the One who exited His own perfect Heaven to sweat and walk and breathe and ache and live on this orb we call home. Unafraid to leave the Holy of holies for the dregs of the earth, He found a way to show us that the earth is the Lord's and everything in it. Everything.

IT IS THE MAGNIFICENT CONTRADICTION THAT GIVES LIFE AND COLOR TO EVERYTHING WE KNOW AND EVERYTHING WE DON'T WANT TO KNOW.

I love to imagine the sight of an eight-year-old Jesus joyfully making angels in the Nazareth snow, knowing full well He could have stayed in heaven and kept on making the real thing.

I love to remember how He let a woman

waste expensive perfume in one lavish aban-
donment to the moment. Or how, out of the
dirt at His feet, he mudpacked the blind man
back into the light.

Nothing was too dirty, too out-of-the-
way, or too taboo for Him not to find a way
to use it to turn the world upside-down.

He is the ultimate collision of black and
white and the extraordinary artist who made
that gray beautiful. I wouldn't trade any of it
for the world.

YOUR WORSHIP ADVENTURE

THINK OF THE MOMENTS IN YOUR OWN LIFE WHERE THE "HEAVENLY"
MIXES WITH THE "EARTHLY." HOW HAS GOD USED THE THINGS
OF THIS WORLD TO SHOW YOU MORE OF HIM?

HOPE

HOPE

"BLESSED ARE THE POOR IN SPIRIT,
FOR THEIRS IS THE KINGDOM OF HEAVEN."

MATTHEW 5:3

Let the River Flow
Darrell Evans

Let the poor man say I am rich in Him
Let the lost man say I am found in Him
And let the river flow
Let the blind man say I can see again
Let the dead man say I am born again

And let the river flow
Let the river flow

Let the river flow
Let the river flow
Holy Spirit, come
Move in power
Let the river flow

TWENTY-SIX

IF YOU DIDN'T KNOW THE HAPPY ENDING TO HIS STORY, YOU'D HAVE TO BELIEVE THAT JOSEPH WAS ONE OF THE UNLUCKIEST SCHLEMIELS IN HISTORY.

In one fell swoop he goes from being Dad's golden boy to booty in a shady trade, worth a few coins and a roadside meal. They say it's always darkest just before the dawn, but Joseph must have spent many a day thinking he was trapped in a never-ending night. Everything that could go wrong, did. Whenever there was a lucky break, he didn't catch it.

Yet there's a moral to his story that gives us all a little hope that in the circle of life, anything can come back around again. For good.

It's like the tale of unlucky George Bailey in *It's a Wonderful Life*. He does everything right only to have life go completely wrong around him. He gives everyone a break, trades his dreams in so everyone else's can come true, and then watches everything he owns slip through his fingers in a heartbreaking string of calamities. But at the end, in that final wonderful toast offered to George when his brother proclaims him "the richest man in town," you know he wasn't talking about the load of money that had just been joyously dumped on the table in front of George.

God's a genius at making lemonade out of lemons— and at sharing His secret with a handful of saints willing to learn. "Where there is hope, there is life" is the beginning of the secret. Joseph languished in pits and prisons but always watched the window for the one ray of light peeking in. George Bailey took it on the chin when life kicked him to the ground,

---

JUST WHEN YOU THINK IT CAN'T GET ANY WORSE— WHEN ALL THE PIECES FALL OUT OF PLACE AND YOU KNOW THERE IS NO WAY ANY GOOD CAN EVER COME OF IT—THAT'S HIS CUE.

---

but it didn't take him long to believe wings and a prayer would pick him back up again.

Just when you think it can't get any worse—when all the pieces fall out of place and you know there is no way any good can ever come of it—that's His cue. He'll take everything you thought went wrong and turn it into one incredible, awe-filled right. You just have to believe it's coming. Wait and hope and then know . . .

It's almost too good to be true. And luck has nothing to do with it.

YOUR WORSHIP ADVENTURE

IMAGINE HOW THE WORLD AND PEOPLE AROUND YOU WOULD BE IF
YOU HAD NEVER BEEN BORN. WRITE A SHORT MEMORY OF YOUR OWN
WONDERFUL LIFE AND CELEBRATE THE GOODNESS OF GOD TO HAVE
ALLOWED YOU TO EXPERIENCE LIFE AND BE A VITAL PRESENCE
IN THE LIVES OF OTHERS.

JOURNAL

KNOW

KNOW

"WHY SHOULD WE HONOR THOSE THAT DIE
UPON THE FIELD OF BATTLE? A MAN MAY SHOW AS
RECKLESS A COURAGE IN ENTERING INTO
THE ABYSS OF HIMSELF."

WILLIAM BUTLER YEATS

Knowing You (All I Once Held Dear)

Graham Kendrick

All I once held dear, built my life upon
All this world reveres and wants to own
All I once sought gain I have counted loss
Spent and worthless now
Compared to this
Knowing You Jesus, knowing You
There is no greater thing
You're my all, You're the best
You're my joy, my righteousness
And I love You Lord

Now my heart's desire is to know You more
To be found in You and known as Yours
To possess by faith what I could not earn
All surpassing gift of righteousness
Oh to know the power of Your risen life
And to know You in Your suffering
To become like You in Your death, my Lord
So with You to live and never die

THEY SAY FAMILIARITY BREEDS CONTEMPT, WHICH, IF TRUE, MAKES YOU WONDER WHY WE WOULD STRIVE TO THE IDEAL OF KNOWING GOD INTIMATELY.

Perhaps we just think we want to know God intimately. It seems to me that coming that close to the Divine should be a more frightening prospect than we make it. There's a recurring theme in most of author Nikos Kazantazkis' novels: Don't ask to know God unless you are prepared for the worst. I'm starting to believe that. Anytime one of the novelist's heroes dares to venture into the abyss of knowing God, he is painfully drawn back first to the abyss of his own dark self. And like fire, the closer he comes to understanding God, the deadlier the encounter.

Which isn't to say we should never embark on that perilous journey. We just need to remember that David found favor as a man after God's own heart, not as a man who had captured it. There must be an infinite, dark moat around God that we have no right to cross, lest we think we are more than we really are. "A God who let us prove his existence would be an idol," wrote Bonhoeffer. And God knows that better than we do.

People who have God completely figured out scare me. People who think they need to explain it to me because they have God completely figured out scare me even more. What scares me most is that they're not scared.

They've got this thing called God completely at their disposal. He is completely known. I scare myself because I know I can turn God into that every day, without even trying.

As simple as our modern religious life has made it to know God, there still must be a moment where we stop to consider that maybe He's not what we've drawn Him to be, but the explosive, infinite, ultimately too-large-to-grasp transcender of time, matter, space, and understanding. Still, instead of tiptoeing toward Him with awe and trembling, we barge into His presence like the drunk at the country club. As if we had the right.

In her book *Holy the Firm,* Annie Dillard described the fear that we've so fearlessly lost: "Churches come at God with an unwarranted air of professionalism . . . as though people in themselves were an appropriate set of creatures to have dealings with God. I often think of the set pieces of the liturgy as certain words which people have successfully addressed to God without their getting killed."

Like Jack Nicholson snarling his famous movie line—"You can't handle the truth"— God knows just how near we can approach before we burn up in His sight. Thankfully, He doles out pieces of Himself in ways we can grasp, dazzling us gradually with His light.

And it is in this tenuous balance that we are left to live. Running away from Him would be hopeless. Running toward Him could cost you your life, your mind, your heart . . . There is a price to pay for desperately seeking Him. It is where even angels fear to tread. Proceed with caution.

David was a man after God's own heart. What drives your
desire to know God more? Is your life consumed with it?
Could you handle any more knowing than you have now?

_____

_____

_____

_____

_____

_____

_____

_____

_____

_____

_____

_____

_____

_____

_____

_____

DAY TWENTY-EIGHT
WALK

"IT IS GOOD TO PRAISE THE LORD AND
MAKE MUSIC TO YOUR NAME, O MOST HIGH,
TO PROCLAIM YOUR LOVE IN THE MORNING AND
YOUR FAITHFULNESS AT NIGHT..."

PSALM 92:1-2

I Will Sing
Don Moen

Lord, You seem so far away
A million miles or more it feels today
And though I haven't lost my faith
I must confess right now
That it's hard for me to pray
But I don't know what to say
And I don't know where to start
But as You give the grace
With all that's in my heart

I will sing, I will praise
Even in my darkest hour
Through the sorrow and the pain
I will sing, I will praise
Lift my hands to honor You
Because Your Word is true
I will sing

I WILL SING

WORDS FROM THE SONGWRITER

DON MOEN

When you're privileged to do what I do, to travel around the country and minister to others through worship, you see a lot of church signs. And depending on what neck of the woods you're in, some signs just don't make a lot of sense. Like the one I saw out in front of a beautiful white clapboard chapel on a state highway in Louisiana. It said, "Today's Sermon: the Word of God." Trouble was, besides the obvious fact that all sermons should be based on the Bible, I passed that sign on a Thursday. That sermon was long finished.

Another sign I saw recently really confused me. It read: "Pot Luck Revival, Sunday-Wednesday." I'm still not sure if that church was having a revival or a four-day buffet.

But one church sign seems to be cropping up more

than others these days: "Sinners welcome here." And every time I see one, I think: "Thank the Lord for just telling it like it is."

The only difference between the sinners inside churches and the sinners outside churches is the amazing grace and forgiveness of God. The saints really are sinners who still fall down, but by the outstretched arm of a merciful God, we get up again. And again.

Trouble is, too many Christians think that they have to be worthy to worship the Lord. Many walk through the work week feeling that God is far away. They don't try to pray because they're not convinced He's listening. And besides, the anger and fear and doubt that consume their thoughts isn't really the stuff you're supposed to tell God about, right?

Few things are farther from the truth. Psalm 145:18 says, "The LORD is near to all who call on him, to all who call on him in truth." You can—in fact, God wants you to—tell Him what you really think. To be honest about what's going on in your life and in your

---

THE SAINTS REALLY ARE SINNERS WHO STILL FALL DOWN, BUT BY THE OUTSTRETCHED ARM OF A MERCIFUL GOD, WE GET UP AGAIN. AND AGAIN.

---

heart. He already knows what's going on anyway, but He longs for you to tell Him all the same.

The reality is that everyone goes through days when we feel God is far away. There's a phoniness in some Christian circles that says you don't admit that. But just look at Psalm 109 where David—the sweet psalmist of

Israel who said, "I will bless the Lord at all times"—tells God all about his fear and doubt, in no uncertain terms. Why is David so bold? Because he couldn't be anything but honest before the Lord. That's what God wants in our worship—our spirit and our truth.

The truth really does set us free. Free to worship with our whole hearts.

"I didn't feel anything the entire day," songwriter Don Moen says of the day "I Will Sing" was breathed into existence. Frustrated, he starting singing while driving and the lyrics just "popped out." In fact, he was unconvinced of the song's validity, and largely forgot about it. A few weeks later, a co-worker's 10-year-old daughter was killed in a car accident. Don remembered the song he had scribbled down, recorded it on a CD, and sent it to the girl's father with a note: "I know you feel like, *Where in the world is God?* but I want to encourage you to sing." The song's honesty and hope have made it an enduring part of Moen's musical legacy. A creative force and gold-selling artist, Don Moen is well known as a musician, songwriter, singer, and worship leader. As Executive Vice President of Creative at Integrity Media, he has had a hand in numerous projects that have helped make the company an industry leader and reach thousands worldwide with tools to bring them "into the manifest presence of God."

NEVER GIVE UP ON LIFE. WHEN YOU FALL, WHAT IS THE HOPE
THAT GETS YOU BACK UP AGAIN?

i - JOURNAL

BECOME

BECOME

"LOVE NEVER FAILS."

1 CORINTHIANS 13:8

Days of Elijah
Robin Mark

These are the days of Elijah
Declaring the Word of the Lord
And these are the days of Your servant Moses
Righteousness being restored
And though these are the days of great trials
Of famine and darkness and sword
Still we are the voice in the desert crying
Prepare ye the way of the Lord

Behold He comes riding on the clouds
Shining like the sun at the trumpet call
Lift your voice, it's the Year of Jubilee
Out of Zion's hill salvation comes

These are the days of Ezekial
The dry bones becoming as flesh
And these are the days of your servant David
Rebuilding a temple of praise
And these are the days of the harvest
The fields are white in Your world
And we are the laborers in Your vineyard
Declaring the Word of the Lord

TWENTY-NINE

IT IS A PRIME SCIENTIFIC PRINCIPLE THAT MATTER CAN NEITHER BE CREATED NOR DESTROYED. It can only be transformed from one state into another. I'd contend the same is true of love. If God is love, then surely all we are and all that is around us—every atom of it—embodies that love. No matter what it has to go through.

You cannot destroy love. You can't even create it. It had to come from the source of love itself, and it slowly but surely seeps its way through every inch and pore of our beings. And through its power, it transforms everything it touches into the workings of His will.

The poets describe this kind of transformation when they watch the beauty of creation. When the sculptor becomes the statue . . . when the singer becomes the song . . . when the dancer becomes the dance . . . this is love

I WORSHIP
because I believe the world is just waiting
to see the people we become when we
live every moment in the wonder of worship.

—*David Jeremiah, Author*

working its magic. This is when God the lover becomes Love itself.

Someone once ventured that perhaps art was "nature speeded up and God slowed down." True art has the ability to magnify and illuminate everything good that the world has to offer—and offers it back to us in one dazzling feast. It also can, in one vivid, albeit fleeting snapshot, still the frighteningly limitless speed of God long enough for us to catch

---

ONLY LOVE CAN EXCEED THE BOUNDS OF OUR LIMITATIONS AND IMAGINATIONS AND BRING TO US THAT FINAL BREATHTAKING REALIZATION: IT WILL NEVER GO AWAY.

---

a glimpse. And all of that power is the same with true love. Only love can exceed the bounds of our limitations and imaginations and bring to us that final breathtaking realization: It will never go away. Love will never leave you. You couldn't shake it if you tried.

A man lashed to a tree. The desperate cry of why. The sun leaving the sky, unable to bear the sight below. The masterwork God painted on that sorry, lonely hill, when all of love seemed forever destroyed. But it was not. It could not be destroyed. And just as He said it would, three days later, love transformed death into one empty tomb of life.

And so we are left with this great hope—that the love in you will forever transform you, whether you struggle in its clutches or bask in its comfort—and that everything dead in you, by that same power, can gloriously rise each new day into the wonderful art of life.

YOUR WORSHIP
ADVENTURE

WHAT ARE YOU STRIVING TO "BECOME" IN YOUR LIFE?
CAN YOU SEE THE PLACES WHERE GOD IS PAINTING AND
MOLDING YOU INTO THAT PERSON?

JOURNAL

WISH

WISH

"FAITH IS A PASSIONATE INTUITION."

WILLIAM WORDSWORTH

Lord, I Lift Your Name On High
Rick Founds

Lord, I lift Your name on high
Lord, I love to sing Your praises
I'm so glad You're in my life
I'm so glad You came to save us

You came from heaven to earth to show the way
From the earth to the cross my debt to pay
From the cross to the grave, from the grave to the sky
Lord, I lift Your name on high

THIRTY

We all gasped in

"AND KISSES ON HER LEGS . . ."

astonishment. My gaggle of friends stood wordlessly as one of our own exited the auto-graph line and read what our favorite author had just written in her book. "What?"

It just didn't seem right. We'd just finished ooohing and aaahing at the wondrous prose this idolized author read aloud from his latest writings. He was a genius. A poet. A master of the language. And, although brilliantly humorous, certainly not so lowbrow as to think such a non sequitur would be funny. I think we were all as crushed as we were confused. Not to mention that we received no provocative messages of the sort in our copies— just a plain old "Blessings" and an autograph. Something was definitely not right here.

We grabbed the book from her for our own look. Ah ha! Turns out our friend had creatively already penned her own little biography on the fly page and titled herself as a "wanderer and seeker on the journey of her life . . ." Our man simply finished the thought with his own flourish. "And blessings on her way . . ." is actually what he wrote, albeit with the scrawly illegibility common to his kind.

We laughed all the way home. And then it became our own coded blessing with a wink. You knew that anytime you were wished kisses on your legs, someone cared enough to beg God's best for you on whatever part of the journey you happened to be on at the time. I still even whisper it to myself sometimes when I need the reminder that He's there.

MAY YOUR COMPANIONS BRING LAUGHTER TO THE JOURNEY.

Turns out the road is really long, with many a winding turn, but no one ever has to walk it alone. He'll be there all along, generously scattering other wanderers across your path to walk through it with you. May that road always rise up to meet you. May your companions bring laughter to the journey. May God always be the One you run not away from, but to . . . and may you ever be wished many kisses on your legs.

YOUR WORSHIP
ADVENTURE

As you continue your journey of worship every day,
remember to watch and write down all the blessings of
each day . . . and to thank the One who gave them to you.

JOURNAL

MAY YOUR
ADVENTURE
CONTINUE . . .